Death, Trust, & Society

Death and Remembrance

A SERIES EDITED BY LIONEL ROTHKRUG, GENERAL EDITOR

Death, Trust, and Society: Mapping Religion and Culture, by Lionel Rothkrug

DEATH, TRUST, & SOCIETY

Mapping Religion & Culture

Lionel Rothkrug

North Atlantic Books
Berkeley, California

Published by
North Atlantic Books
P.O. Box 12327
Berkeley, California 94712
www.northatlanticbooks.com

Book design by Susan Quasha
Printed in the United States of America
Distributed to the book trade by Publishers Group West

Death, Trust, and Society: Mapping Religion and Culture is sponsored by the Society for the Study of Native Arts and Sciences, a nonprofit educational corporation whose goals are to develop an educational and crosscultural perspective linking various scientific, social, and artistic fields; to nurture a holistic view of arts, sciences, humanities, and healing; and to publish and distribute literature on the relationship of mind, body, and nature.

Library of Congress Cataloging-in-Publication Data

Rothkrug, Lionel, 1927–
   Death, trust, and society : mapping religion and culture / by Lionel Rothkrug.
      p. cm. — (Death and remembrance ; 1)
   Summary: "A cross-cultural study of how religious practices—particular attitudes toward the dead seen in funerary rites, mortuary practices, and pilgrimage patterns—have influenced the formation of cultural identity and social structures throughout world history"—Provided by the publisher.
   ISBN 1-55643-551-7 (trade cloth)
   1. Death—Religious aspects—Comparative studies. 2. Death—Cross-cultural studies. I. Title. II. Series.

BL504.R68 2006
203'.88—dc22

2005033101

1 2 3 4 5 6 7 DATA 10 09 08 07 06

For Anne

Contents

About the Series

In the series Death and Remembrance, each book will take as its point of departure the general theory set forth in this initial volume. Collectivities, like individuals, progress from infancy to maturity in differentiated stages. Just as childhood experiences influence the formation of an adult personality so too do attitudes shown toward the dead (as in funerary rites, mortuary practices, and patterns of pilgrimage) shape the formation of social structures in a society's early formative period and influence the development of cultural traits. "The organization of an individual's powers to behave" defines a human personality in much the same way as a society or collectivity acquires personality in the exercise of its organizational activity.

In highly integrated nations, where ritual recognition of non-kin dead goes back to an early historical period, popular pilgrimage to tombs of holy persons promoted feelings of intimacy with previous generations and established a strong sense of human connectedness among the faithful. Pilgrims who sought to stand in the presence of the sanctified dead also believed the society itself was collective being, alive and also prior to all its living members. In sum, portable forms of sanctity engendered high levels of trust among the living and promoted strong feelings of reverence toward non-kin dead. Meanwhile, in lands where sanctity was fixed and pilgrimage was rare, few people offered prayers for the benefit of non-kin dead. People fear strangers, are haunted by evil spirits, and widespread popular distrust seriously diminishes socio-cultural coherence.

Several scholars have applied this theory to study of religious practices in specific countries. Among the works in progress that I hope to include in this series are investigations of religious Fundamentalism in the United States; the history of cults to the Virgin Mary in Meso-America during the century following the arrival of the Conquistadors; early German peregrinations to the Holy Land; the evolution of Japanese religious practices associated with pilgrimage; the high levels of portable sanctity in early modern Japan; and the various forms of Chinese ritual practices, including the link between fixed forms of sanctity and the proliferation of demonic beings in China.

Lionel Rothkrug

Acknowledgments

In the course of four decades many people and several institutions helped me in researching and writing this book. During each decade I focused the work on a different culture.

Seventeenth-century France was the first area in which I did sustained research. The late Professors William J. Bouwsma at the University of California in Berkeley, and Jean Meuvret of the *École Practiques des Hautes Etúdes* in Paris guided me through the labyrinths of the national, provincial, and notarial archives. In the course of this work, Professor Meuvret taught me to think of the dead as merely "another age group."

In the 1980s I turned to the distribution of pilgrimage shrines in late medieval and Reformation Germany. This enterprise could never have been accomplished without financial aid from the *Deutsche Forschungsgemeinschaft* and scholarly direction from the late Professor Karl Bosl in Munich and from the late George Hunston Williams, Hollis Professor of Divinity at Harvard University. Ingrid Scheidt helped me gather and map the distribution of German pilgrimage shrines prior to the Reformation. Her heroic contribution was of great assistance in this very difficult task.

Since then Professor Lewis Lancaster, founder of Buddhist Studies at the University of California in Berkeley, encouraged me to use the same methods in the study of religious practices and attitudes toward the dead in the lands associated with the Silk Road, the trade routes connecting ancient Rome with China. Professor Lancaster enlisted numerous scholars to help me in this enterprise. They include Professor Mark Blum, at the State University of New York in Albany; Professor Whalen Lai, at the University of California in Davis; and Professor Phyllis Jestice at the University of Southern Mississippi. Additionally, David Bundy, Librarian at the Christian Theological Seminary, and Bruce Williams, Research Librarian at the East Asian Library at the University of California in Berkeley, along with Hollis Meyer-deLancey, gave many helpful comments and valuable suggestions in formulating this general theory of mapping religion and culture.

Without Anne Poley's constant encouragement and unflagging support I could not have completed this work. Also, I am grateful for the various types of assistance generously given by Anne Gregersen, Joyce Slater, Linda Oppen, Ada Carty, Jessie DeMaio, and Cliff and Sherry Frost.

Finally, special thanks are owed to Julie Brand and Kathy Glass, my editors at North Atlantic Books.

Introduction

THIS STUDY DISCUSSES THE influence of religious practices on patterns of cultural development. Several arguments advanced here are formulated to allow computer-generated maps to verify the cross-cultural evidence recurrently adduced in support of a general theory of how religion relates to social structure. The implications that may follow from this cartographical approach are described toward the end of this introduction. The theory rests on a single premise: collectivities, like individuals, progress from infancy to maturity in differentiated stages. Just as a successful passage from one age group to another constitutes a so-called normal development for an individual, so a history of progressively higher levels of socio-cultural coherence signifies an optimal evolution for a society. Childhood experiences influence the formation of adult personality in much the same way that attitudes shown toward the dead in early historical periods—seen in funerary rites, mortuary practices, and pilgrimage patterns—shape the formation of social structures and contribute to the development of cultural traits.

The proposed parallel between factors contributing to the formation of individual and collective identities is not offered as a mere rhetorically constructed resemblance. The analogy follows from an established sociological principle. Just as "the organization of an individual's powers to behave" defines a human being's personality,[1] so too does a society acquire personality in the exercise of its organizational activity. And the frequency of figural or typological speech largely determines the organizational powers of individual and collective behavior. As a distinguished archeologist points out,

> metaphor often provides the simplest or most parsimonious
> means of communication between socialized individuals in the
> same culture. To describe the actions of a person as those of a

fox or a viper, through commonly held cultural conventions of the connotations of a fox or a viper, can be a very succinct way of conveying information about him or her. Through metaphorical means it becomes possible to convey complex configurations of ideas with a very few words. Many metaphors cannot be paraphrased in a literal language. Often either a metaphor is used or nothing can be said.[2]

In some societies, however, ritual supplants speech. Consider the following passage from a book entitled *State and Court Ritual in China:*

> Confucians early on stressed how ritual could replace language and so create harmony; one can argue with a speech, but how can one reply to a ritual act except in the affirmative? …
>
> Ritual also fostered harmony by obliging people to shut up. Its coercive power might have imposed unwelcomed restrictions on emperors, officials and court personnel, limiting their scope of action far more effectively than any set of laws. But, these men soon found the silence (or restricted use of language) in a ritual performance a useful way of communicating their views and ideas, particularly when they feared that recourse to explicit oral or written language might prove too risky or disruptive.[3]

Behavioral incoherence is endemic in societies where ritual supplants speech in the governing of society.

Rituals are of course universal. Those rites and ceremonies associated with portable forms of sanctity foster high levels of behavioral coherence, and contribute to a wider use of figurative expression. Conversely, a fragmentation of ritual practices and an endemic state of cultic disunity prevails in societies where sanctity is either rooted in the earth or largely immobilized. Thus, a paucity of figurative expression and inadequate behavioral coherence in Imperial China are closely correlated with the numerous societal disabilities flowing from fixed forms of sanctity, namely: cultic disunity, poor political integration, separatism, social discordance, and a general lack of trust.

In this context, notions of *sanctity* are important. One usage refers to the supernatural powers ascribed by pilgrims to the tombs of saints—as, for example, in medieval France, in England, and in Japan. This type of sanctity is portable; and it fostered intimate relations between the living and the dead. At issue here is the term *devotion,* meaning religious worship or observance. The word refers both to an *act* and to the *exercise* of worship. Only the exercise of devotion has emotional content; the act itself is devoid of subjective feelings. Thus the figurative expression dominant in the songs sung and the stories recounted by a group of pilgrims proceeds from the collective exercise of devotion. In contrast, consider the patterns of avoidance associated with funerary practices in Imperial China. At this time "a classic ritual prescribed that the [deceased individual] with its physical remains should be enshrined in a fixed location and be mourned only by its own kin and kind."[4] Sanctity was rooted at the tombs where people offered blood sacrifices to their forbears. These rituals were believed to placate angry ancestors and keep demonic spirits at bay. The oblations had no devotional content. In sum, a multitude of isolated ancestor cults blurred the character of China's collective personality, impaired the society's ability to organize its behavior, and severely limited the use of figurative expression in ordinary discourse.

The United States: Portable Sanctity and the Forgotten Dead

In predominantly Protestant societies, especially in the United States, people emphatically dissociated the dead from a remarkably mobile type of sanctity. European immigrants who entered North America in the seventeenth and eighteenth centuries, mostly Protestants, ascribed sanctity to the Bible, not to the dead. In fact, many pious Protestants believed that departed souls required no ritual recognition. Puritans and a majority of Baptists, as well as other extreme Calvinists, even refused to read Scriptural passages at funeral ceremonies. A simple interment without religious service qualified as a "decent burial." A dearth of mortuary rituals among many sectors of the Protestant population helps to explain, for example, why anthropologists find that "we have more descriptive material about funerals in Indonesia than in America.... Nowhere [in the United States] do we have an ethnography of death."[5]

The Bible, at once eminently portable and also the sole source of sanctity, allowed public preachers to disseminate God's word throughout the colonized lands. In North America the title "Pilgrim"—first ascribed to Protestant separatists residing in the Plymouth colony—may also apply in a figurative sense to the early Protestant immigrants who listened to itinerant preachers declaiming the Lord's message in one community after another. In the mid nineteenth century opposition to a widespread system of chattel slavery led to the Civil War; and years of armed hostilities deepened the population's estrangement from departed souls. Toward the end of that epic conflict, Abraham Lincoln's Gettysburg Address (November 1863) and his appointment of a *national* day of Thanksgiving in the same year helped to nationalize the dead; and the federal movement to restore political unity also nationalized America's cultural heritage. Literary works written before the defeat of separatism rapidly became viewed as a national literature; and the historicity of these writings helped to create a collective memory transcending regional boundaries. Gary Wills has elegantly summarized the dramatic effect of the 272 words Lincoln pronounced on the battlefield at Gettysburg:

> What had been a mere theory of lawyers like James Wilson, Joseph Story, and Daniel Webster—that the nation preceded the states, in time and importance—now became a lived reality of American tradition.... Up to the Civil War, "The United States" was invariably a plural noun: "The United States are a free government." After Gettysburg, it became a singular: "The United States is a free government."[6]

To be sure, Gettysburg was the first national burial ground. Yet at no time did national memorials and a correspondingly pervasive national culture give rise to a nation-wide consciousness of a common dead. Quite the contrary, northerners and southerners established separate memorials to their own fallen soldiers. Meanwhile, deceased slaves and freedmen, many of whom had fought in support of the Union forces, were largely forgotten. A geographical dispersion of their descendants in the aftermath of the Civil War, however, has a curious parallel in the earlier history of the approximately six hundred Indian tribes who inhabited various parts of North America when the first European explorers arrived on the continent. Many tribes had descended from an ancient population known as Mound Builders. "Their mounds, which served as foundations for temples and dwellings, as fortifications, as burial chambers and as religious sites and totems, varied in size from 1 to 100 acres." The European advance into the American interior "eventually eradicated all remnants of this mound-building culture."[7]

The disappearance of virtually every trace of the ancient mound-building culture and subsequently, many centuries later, a scattering of a relatively small number of Indian tribes across vast land areas left most regions in North America without any places notable for trans-local traditions. To be sure, Indian "Nations" inhabited specific territories. But the European colonists who occupied Indian territories encountered no people with indigenous traditions hindering them from ultimately establishing a vast system of chattel slavery. In the eighteenth century human life did not own itself among the large numbers of slaves who were sold on the auction block. Chattel slaves did not participate in the evolution of humanity. The first symbolic recognition that African American soldiers and sailors are to be counted among the dead deserving of a national rite of remembrance is the memorial dedicated on November 10, 1984, to the service men and women slain in the Vietnam War.

The monument also marks a moment when for the first time the government invested large sums of money to find, identify, and return the bodily remains of the war-dead, either to the family relatives or to inter them in a national cemetery. Prior to this date soldiers slain in foreign wars were buried abroad. The approximate temporal coincidence between establishing a memorial to the slain in Vietnam and a truly national reclamation of American war-dead is a practice reminiscent of ancient Greek funeral orations.[8] At that time, the entire citizen body gathered to hear the orations performed amid the reclaimed bodies of fallen soldiers. These solemnities testify to the close relation between a historical consciousness and public ceremonies recognizing a common dead.

Such traditions never took root in the United States. A traditional indifference to religious services for the dead among many Protestants and the different funerary services held for those slain in the Civil War not only deprived the country of a common dead, but the failure to recognize a common dead also explains why episodes of pandemic distrust have acquired increasing notoriety in the United States since World War II. No low-trust society has a common dead, and the United States offers no exception to this general rule. The witch hunt led by Senator Joseph McCarthy—head of the Congressional Committee for un-American Activities—was perhaps the earliest and certainly the most notorious post-war manifestation of political paranoia. McCarthy and his committee ruined the careers of many professional people who were innocent of any wrongdoing. The same witch-hunt mentality also dominated the White House during the real and alleged conspiracies associated with the Watergate scandals and the events leading to the resignation of President Richard Nixon. Much the same seems to be true of President Ronald Reagan. According to Eli Sagan,

> The mirror image of the conspirators and traitors within a society is the picture of the cunning, near-omnipotent enemies without, who have to be constantly defended against. The manifestation vis-à-vis the external world of the paranoid person's continuous, rigidly maintained directedness of himself is a continuous and preoccupying concern with the defense of his autonomy against external assault. There is a consistent attempt to magnify the power and the cunning of the outside enemy, the "evil empire" of former President Ronald Reagan's fairly recent paranoid parry.[9]

The utterly insane Oklahoma City bombing committed by two ordinary citizens on April 19, 1995—and the many corporate abominations made public since the mid-1990s—suggests that the long history of paranoia in government had finally become ubiquitous in the general population. To cite an anonymous dictum, "America has become a storefront for a corporate mob."[10] Public figures now openly lament the general dearth of trust. But the winters of discontent they declaim merely confirm that the most powerful low-trust society on Earth possesses minimal levels of socio-cultural coherence. As a distinguished sociologist put it,

> Unless the members of a society share a set of core values, internalizing them in their personalities and having them further reinforced by social rites and institutions, social order will be unreliable.[11]

Endemic distrust in the United States may be attributed to the fact that this country never possessed a common dead, not even in colonial times—a fact confirmed by Thomas Jefferson's vehement assertion that the dead do not exist in the eyes of the living. Jefferson's dictum—cited toward the end of the Introduction—suggests that our contemporary dilemmas may have distant and truly unsuspected origins. At this point it may be helpful to repeat a passage and citation appearing on the first page of this essay. Just as "the organization of an individual's powers to behave" defines a human being's personality, so a society acquires personality in the exercise of its organizational activity. This parallel, taken from an established sociological principle, is reiterated here to argue that levels of identity correlate closely with the measure of conscious behavioral control among both individuals and societies. Freud's concept of the unconscious—that an individual has within him activities of which he is not aware—has a parallel with the hidden historical origins of collective behavior. In other words, psychology may offer evidence about the causes of political paranoia in contemporary America. As one scholar points out,

> Human beings have always talked of "dark powers" forcing them to do things they did not intend; making them embark on hopeless or incomprehensible missions in spite of themselves. Most religions are grounded in some notion of invisible powers in which one nevertheless believes, as are many myths. The idea

of the unknown or unknowable in the mind of humankind is not a new one, and the concept of an unconscious can be made to dovetail nicely with certain theological beliefs.[12]

The perception of our national personality is at issue here. The United States defines its personality by the nation's organizational activity; and the figure of Uncle Sam represents this personality. Symbolic portrayals of England, France, and the United States as human beings—known respectively as John Bull, Marie France, and Uncle Sam—all possess distinctive personality traits. Since these images, called "organological analogies," are clearly distinguishable from one another, our task is to identify the personality traits that are unique to Uncle Sam.[13] Historically, the image appears most frequently on the familiar "I Want You" military recruiting posters. Toward the end of the Civil War, when Lincoln's Gettysburg Address and his appointment of a *national* day of Thanksgiving in the same year represented measures to restore political unity and to recognize a national dead, many people believed that the figure of Uncle Sam represented the nation. In the nineteenth century, however, Uncle Sam did not represent the United States in the same ways as John Bull and Marie France represented their respective nations. For John Bull had never been designated as an uncle; nor did Marie France ever appear as an aunt.

Quite the contrary, John Bull and Marie France are figures possessing first and last names that represent *all* the peoples of the nations they personify. In contrast, the appellation *Sam* is a familiar form of a first name. Moreover, the intimacy suggested by this sobriquet is preceded by the designation *Uncle,* signifying a close family relative. Any allegedly *national* character ascribed to the icon, therefore, is contradicted by the family reference to an *Uncle.* In sum, the image equates a preferred social status with full citizenship. The first major effort to truly democratize the dead, and to abolish the preferential connotations associated with images of Uncle Sam, appears in an annual ritual, known for the calling-out of every slain soldier's name inscribed on the Vietnam Memorial. The ceremony helps to transform Uncle Sam into everybody's uncle; and, for that reason, this ritual constitutes a major step toward creating a truly national symbol, or organological analogy, representing all the people of the United States.

Civil War, Nationhood, and the Rise of Evangelical Religions

His study of the lives of Thomas Jefferson and Abraham Lincoln, explains author Christopher Hitchens, allowed him "to consider and reconsider the whole idea of the United States *ab initio.*"[14] Lincoln's address at Gettysburg begins with a chronological attribution—"four score and seven years ago"—to the Declaration of Independence, not to the Constitution. The remaining words in the sentence—"our fathers brought forth on this continent a new nation, conceived in Liberty and dedicated to the proposition that all men are created equal"—refers to "the rights of man" and to Jefferson's espousal of a "free right to the unbounded exercise of reason and freedom of opinion."

Enlightened leaders and liberal deists did not foresee that the Revolution would inspire countless numbers of ordinary people—most of them with little education—"to create new egalitarian and emotionally satisfying evangelical communities." While virtually all of the

> …major colonial churches either declined or failed to gain relative to other groups in the years between 1760 and 1790, Methodist and Baptist congregations grew by leaps and bounds. The Baptists expanded from 94 congregations in 1760 to 858 in 1790 to become the single largest denomination in America.… By 1790 [the Methodists] had created over 700 congregations to rival in numbers the older Congregational and Presbyterian churches. It would not be long before the Methodists, organized nationally into circuits and locally into classes and served by uneducated itinerant preachers, became the largest Church in America.[15]

As mentioned earlier, the immensely popular movements that make up the "religious right" today—many of them going back to the late eighteenth century—do not recognize a common dead. Indeed, "born again" evangelical Christians stress the "importance of the Armageddon and the role of the Jews in the Second Coming of Christ. Pre-millennial Fundamentalists not only look forward to the establishment of the 'Kingdom of God' on the Davidic throne of Jerusalem; they also hope to be physically 'raptured' to heaven when the Jews return to Israel."[16] In contrast, a movement toward establishing a common dead—beginning with the dedication of the Vietnam Memorial in 1984—has been supplemented both by ceremonies to memorialize the victims of terrorist attacks on September 11, 2001, and also by the continuous return of the bodies of military personnel and civilians from the wars in Afghanistan and Iraq. There seems to be a direct correlation between a growing popular recognition of the people who die in public service associated with warfare, and the increasing militancy of present-day evangelicals.

Religious Practices and the Formation of Collective and Personal Identities

To say that collective and individual *identity* reflect traits associated with either a fixed or a portable mode of sanctity is to assert that these two types of sanctity are also manifested in collective and individual forms of *personality;* and both are the product of religious practices. Sanctity was rooted at the tombs where people offered blood sacrifices to their forbears in Imperial China. Throughout the medieval and early modern periods these oblations—which served to keep angry ancestors and demonic spirits at bay—were an essential feature of a family religion that prevailed amid widespread popular and public participation in Confucian, Buddhist, and Taoist rituals.

A traditional division between the observance of a *private* religion to sustain historic family lineages and a simultaneous performance of *public* rites and festivals to advance the welfare of the living in this world and the next tells us, among many other things, that religious rituals are not always associated with religious belief. As one scholar puts it,

> For the Chinese, religion is a matter of practices and festivals, rather than a belief-oriented system; and Chinese culture is influenced by three different teaching systems, Confucian, Buddhist, and Taoist.... Thus the teachings of Confucius are guidelines for social behavior, Buddhism for the afterlife, and Taoism for relations between the human body and nature. There is no contradiction in the Chinese mind, in practicing all three of these systems at once.[17]

Thus, a ubiquitous family religion stood apart and remained totally isolated from institutions that exercised different forms of trans-kin authority. On the one hand, therefore, an exclusion of ancestor cults from huge areas of trans-kin jurisdiction effectively perpetuated the dispersion of the family dead among vast numbers of ancestral tombs. And, on the other hand, the absence of an effective system of trans-kin authority radically reduced the organization of the society's powers, and thereby deprived the empire of well-defined personality traits.

The indistinct features of China's collective personality, a collective identity blurred by a multitude of isolated ancestor cults, profoundly affected the nature of discourse. The Chinese believed the blood sacrifices they offered at family tombs had apotropaic powers, that is, they could avert contamination, dispel evil, and avoid ill luck. People who were engaged in these rites rarely gave voice to figurative expression. A distinguished scholar of world literature explains that "consciousness must be understood in both its *intentionalist* and *participatory* modes."[18] Applying this principle to Imperial China, it is clear that the actors' consciousness of participation in ancestor cults was largely limited to the family group; and since blood sacrifices offered to deceased family members were ritual acts of avoidance, the sense of intentionality increased along with a corresponding suppression of figurative expression. Conversely, in countries where pilgrims visited tombs of deceased holy persons, the prayers and thanksgivings they delivered, which abounded in metaphors, conflated pious intentions with participation in communal devotions. And the same sense of participation is also prominent in the songs and stories that raised pilgrims' spirits in their travels to distant shrines.

Devotional acts may be individual or collective. For example, songs and stories sung by a group of pilgrims constitute a *collective* act of devotion. These communal expressions of religious aspiration point to a correlation between portable modes of sanctity and the rise of literature. And the relation between pilgrimage and literary development is by no means confined to the West. Scholarly writings on this topic are diverse. A work describing the influence of religious peregrination on European literature,[19] and another book about similar phenomena in Japan and France,[20] are studies which, when taken together, remind us that the feeling-informed images voiced on journeys to the tombs of saints occasionally resembled the verbal imagery so prominent in conversations carried on with deceased persons in dreams—a practice known as *muchu mondo* in medieval Japan.[21]

Two themes are at issue here. The first is geographic. In the opening paragraph of this introduction, I asserted that electronically generated maps showing an approximate regional distribution of figurative expression in the histories of different societies would reveal at a glance more information about comparative cultural development than one might gather from months, perhaps even years of reading. Similarly, the second subject area also has a geographical dimension. The personalities and the states of mind ascribed to characters in the literary works mentioned above were created in lands possessing portable forms of sanctity; and they reflect the attitudes and cultural traits prominent in societies possessing a common dead. The fact that specialists in Chinese studies seem unable to find a single pre-modern writing that describes an individual's *subjective* state of mind points, once again, to the dispersion of the Chinese dead and to a corresponding paucity of an inter-subjective experience that transcends regional differences.

To describe someone's state of mind, even that of a fictional character, is a task performed most readily in a social environment notable for relatively easy interactions among people who are unknown to one another. The high levels of trust typical of such a society allow for an interpersonal behavior in which the actors have an awareness of both the *intention-alist* and the *participatory* aspects of consciousness. This double-sided cognizance, the source of our inter-subjective experience, was seriously impaired by the propitiatory intent of funerary services performed at family graves in Imperial China. These rituals, designed to ward off ghosts and demonic spirits, imbued the living with deep suspicions of strangers. This is why, when scholars compare Chinese and Japanese literature, they find early Japanese writings to be unique. The autobiographies in diary form surviving from the Heian period (794–1145) are judged to be "marvels of world literature."[22]

In sum, fixed sanctity and a widespread ritual avoidance of ghosts and evil spirits correlates closely with a pervasive fear of strangers; and this apprehension is the chief mark of a low-trust society. Conversely, the dead are invariably viewed as beneficent in lands where sanctity is portable and where a plenitude of deceased holy persons are interred at pilgrimage sites. In these societies, where an abundance of miracle stories laid the foundation for a subsequent rise of a national literature, pilgrimage correlated closely with a widespread development of trust. According to Chaucer's *Canterbury Tales*, pilgrims often traveled in groups formed by people who had hitherto stood as strangers toward each other. The decision to travel as a single community ensured everyone of a proper burial in the event of a death during the pilgrimage; and pilgrims in Japan also arranged for similar guarantees. Many centuries of popular religious peregrination eventually established a common trust among large sectors of the English and Japanese populations. The close ties established among pilgrims assumed an even wider public dimension when—as is recounted in the *Canterbury Tales* and in comparable stories from Japan—strangers frequently befriended pilgrims. These people believed they participated, and thereby indirectly shared, in the pilgrim's progress toward an ultimate redemption. Today high-trust societies, such as England, France, and Japan, are notable for long histories of nation-wide and, in many instances, even international peregrination to reliquary shrines.

Ultimately, the vast numbers of pilgrims who for many centuries continued to travel to the tombs of saints—along with those who died in these journeys—established memorials and entered into common communion with departed souls. Among other things, ritual communication with the dead imparted a shared sense of temporal continuity among the living. The belief that past and present generations participated in creating a common destiny allowed people to internalize social norms. From an observer's perspective the communal assimilation of social norms is essential to the formation of a collective identity. But adoption and adaptation of normative criteria was an exceedingly gradual process. In earlier times people equated collective identity with a unified consciousness that included previous generations. For example, Richard Hooker (1554–1600), who believed that the living and the dead stand in contractual relations toward one another, a view entirely consistent with Common Law tradition, wrote the following passage:

> Of this pointe therefore we are to note, that sith men naturally have no ful and perfect power to commande whole politique multitudes of men; therefore utterly without our consent we could in such sort be at no mans commandment living. And to be commanded we do consent, when that societie whereof we are a parte hath at any time before consented, without revoking the same by the like universal agreement. Wherefore any man's deed past is good as long as him selfe continueth: so the act of a public societie of men done five hundred yeares sithence standeth as theirs, who presently are of the same societies, *because corporations are immortall: we were then alive in our predecessors, and they in their successors do live still.*[23]

In sum, a multitude of associations performed numerous devotional activities. The pilgrimages, mortuary rites, communal prayers, and memorial services performed in the public domain were largely replicated in confraternities. Ultimately, the abundance of pious activities eventually established an almost universal participation in ritually enacted communion with previous generations. The citation from Richard Hooker shows that an expansion of communal intimacy with the dead over many centuries ultimately led people to associate the notion of trust with the meaning they ascribed to the word *public*. Prayers at the tombs of holy persons not only gave rise to institutions of *public* memorial, but an age-old tradition of burials *ad sanctos* also transmitted common feelings from one generation to the next. Among other things, this long record of unbroken communion with previous generations—a history providing the subject matter for much medieval prose and poetry—eventually gave rise to a national literature. Intimacy with non-kin dead fostered a sense of human connectedness; and it is worth repeating that membership in a society thought to be prior to all its living inhabitants made people aware of the simultaneity of the *intentionalist* and the *participatory* aspects of consciousness.

The organological analogies mentioned earlier show that a society will have *both* identity *and* a personality—formed largely by internalized social norms—in the measure that it possesses a sameness which is at once trans-generational and also sufficiently coherent to obscure the boundaries indicating where the community leaves off and the individual begins. Circumstances or policies that curtail ritual interchange with previous generations weaken socio-cultural coherence, dampen hopes of redemption, and reduce the frequency of figurative speech able to give voice to common feelings. And, above all, the alienation of departed souls drastically diminishes trust among individuals unrelated by kinship.

CHAPTER I

•◆•

Immanence and Language in the Formation
of Individual and Collective Identity

I~~N THE INTRODUCTION~~ I argued that the correlation between an absence of a common dead and diminished abilities to develop collective and individual identity originates in the failure of a people to interiorize social norms. Thus, personality traits acquire definition in the measure that individuals and collectivities effectively organize their respective powers to behave; while, at the same time, internalization of social norms correlates closely with the presence of a common dead. Also important is a distinction between a mere capacity of an individual or a collectivity to organize outward activities, and the actual performance of these activities. Rules cannot be internalized in the absence of performance. To say that personality is revealed in an individual's behavior is to recognize, on the one hand, that personal behavior is conditioned by the ability to interiorize social norms; and, on the other, to acknowledge that interiorized norms shape the character of religious practices.

In his important book *Religion and Regime,* Guy E. Swanson uses the term *immanence* to describe human perceptions of spiritual influences. In his view *immanence* is

> an intimate influencing of one spirit by another, the influence occurring through the actual transfer of a power from one spirit to another. The transferred attribute merges with those already present in the spirit receiving it.[1]

Levels of immanence reflect different degrees of social organization. In Europe, for example, the powers perceived to be immanent in the relics of saints during the early Middle Ages had not nearly the potency subsequently ascribed to the body and blood of Christ conveyed to the believer in the Eucharist ceremony. In 1215, the Fourth Lateran Council used the current term *transubstantiation* to assert the *Real Presence*—the identity of Christ's Eucharistic body with His Body in Heaven. The level of thought and the sophistication reflected in the writings of Thomas Aquinas (1225–1274), in which he worked out the details of Eucharistic doctrine, were largely absent from the writings composed in the early Middle Ages. At that time the immanence residing in literary and religious texts corresponded to the primitive level of the immanence reflected in a multitude of localized relic cults.

The development of literature and philosophy—evident, for example, in the recovery of Aristotelian texts, possibly including his *Poetics*—was an essential factor in creating the conditions for the institutionalization of Christ's immanence in the Eucharistic body. Immanence in language usage resides in the evocation of sentiments that possess both intentional and participatory qualities, a state of mind that Eric Voegelin has called "the paradox of consciousness." As one author describes Voegelin's views,

> Consciousness intends objects, and in this capacity of intentionality, reality consists of "things" intended by a bodily located (and thus "thingly") consciousness, of what Voegelin calls "thing reality" (Laozi's "ten thousand things"). But a thinker will be engaging in an act of imaginative oblivion if she or he takes thing-reality for the whole picture because consciousness has its participatory dimension as well…. Intentional acts always occur within a comprehending structure of reality.[2]

Mark Johnson has discussed these matters at length in a book entitled, *The Body in the Mind: The Bodily Basis of Meaning, Imagination, and Reason*.[3] Arguing against a prevailing "Objectivism" in theories of meaning and rationality, Johnson locates powers of imagination in human embodiment. Among many other things, he shows that the human embodiment of understanding may be seen in the simple fact that human experience reflects the history of semantic changes in many world languages.[4] Seen from this perspective, metaphor is conceived as

> a pervasive mode of understanding by which we project patterns from one domain of experience in order to structure another domain of a different kind. So conceived metaphor is not merely a linguistic mode of expression; rather, it is one of the chief cognitive structures by which we are able to have coherent ordered experiences that we can reason about and make sense of.... Understanding via metaphorical projection from the concrete to the abstract makes use of physical experiences in two ways. First, our bodily movements and interactions in various physical domains of experience are structured (as we saw with image schemata), and that structure can be projected by metaphor onto abstract domains. Second ... Concrete bodily experience not only constrains the "input" to the metaphorical projections, but also the nature of the projections themselves, that is, the kinds of mappings that can occur across domains.[5]

If Eric Voegelin's idea of consciousness—as "subject intending objects" located in a participatory field—had a temporal dimension, his concept would be consistent with Johnson's view that the history of semantic changes in language manifests a movement whereby metaphor transports human understanding from the more concrete and physical toward the more abstract and nonphysical. Much the same process applies to the realm of Buddhist-inspired aesthetics in Japan. Consider, for example, Jeff Humphries' comments about the artistic and literary perceptions of bonsai trees, first brought to Japan by Buddhist monks from China. Kyozo Murata, a great contemporary bonsai master, has defined the art form thus:

> Bonsai is a living plant transferred to a pot or tray or a rock or a stone so that it can continue to live semi-permanently. It has not only a natural beauty of the particular plant but the appearance reminds people *of something other than the plant*

itself. It could be a scene, a forest, or part of a forest, a lone tree in the field, a seascape, a lake, a river or a stream or a pond. It is also possible that a certain appearance reminds a person of the wind blowing through the branches.[6]

"The art of bonsai," explains Humphries, "seeks to achieve a wordless state of spatial and temporal transcendence *within the ordinariness of space and time*—a kind of *transcendence through immanence,* achieving askesis by immersion in the everyday"[7] (Humphries' italics). To achieve transcendence through immanence required no rituals; and this ultimate state of awareness was accessible to every human being. The following lines by a fourteenth-century Japanese Zen priest, garden designer, and poet also emphasize the wordless meanings acquired when one is aware of a transcendent immanence: The sounds of the stream

> splash out
>
>> the Buddha's sermon
>
> Don't say
>
>> that the deepest meaning
>>
>>> comes only from one's mouth
>
> Day and night
>
>> eighty thousand poems
>>
>>> arise one after the other
>
>> and in fact
>>
>> not a single word
>> has ever been spoken.[8]

A long history of a democratized dead, largely brought about by the Buddhist concern for departed souls, allowed transcendence through immanence to be widely accessible in modern Japan.

Many factors apart from the absence of a common dead help to explain why the verses cited above are inconceivable in modern China. A literature develops over time; but the peoples of Japan and China understood their past in very different ways. Many aspects of Japanese history may be seen in the monuments and artifacts that mark historical events and reflect earlier styles of life. In contrast, China's representation of the past resides largely in its language. In an earlier age, when the Chinese embodied their emotions, people could not easily verbalize their feelings. Similarly, today ordinary folks tend to personify the past by speaking and writing in the language of antiquity. For example, advertisements for washing machines, toothpaste, and televisions displayed along the streets "are expressed in a written language that has remained practically unchanged for the last two thousand years. In kindergarten toddlers chant Tang poems that were written two thousand years ago." Yet, continues Pierre Ryckmans,[9] "this same China which is loaded with so much history and so many memories is oddly deprived of ancient monuments." Most Chinese cities— including those which were ancient capital-cities or prestigious cultural centers—are "strangely devoid of all traditional character."[10] Put simply, history is inherited; and today, the embodiment of an ancient language in daily life functions as a universal representation of a previous age. No cultural traits could be more incompatible with the poems and works of art that induce "a wordless state of spatial and temporal transcendence."

The Japanese were acutely aware of this cultural incompatibility with China during the Heian period (794–1185). At that time, "classical Chinese was the perfect handmaiden of Chinese historiography, or rather, they continued to reinforce each other. The reticence and impersonality of Chinese historical discourse are fully in accord with the terseness, the selectivity, and uniformity of classical Chinese. Narrative economy unites the two."[11] Today, explains Pei-Yi Wu, autobiography is a literary genre much closer to the opposite pole. At the beginning of his work, however, Pei-Yi Wu expresses his admiration for the Japanese autobiographies in diary form surviving from the Heian period. Declaring these works to be "marvels of world literature," he points out that "scholars today are still puzzling over the suddenness of their efflorescence. Nowhere else in the world at that time or even in the next five or six centuries was there such a vivid description of daily life, a free and easy avowal of feeling and thought, or leisurely, unhurried pace of narration. In her sharpness of observation and fine-scale representation Sei Shonagon [a Japanese lady autobiographer] was a true sister of Katherine Mansfield."[12]

These masterpieces appeared in a period when kings retired as monks. Just as the Heian court gave public recognition to the diaries produced under its oversight, so the monastic status of retired monarchs gave royal recognition to the bestowal of Buddhist names to ordinary people at their burial. A national literature appeared amid a democratization of death. The scriptural character of Buddhist teachings, and widespread popular pilgrimage to the tombs of holy persons—a practice supplemented by itinerant holy men, called *hijiri,* who buried and performed last rites for the abandoned dead—all converged to create a close connection between establishing a national literature and universalizing the right to a proper burial.

To put these views about the public character of death and narration in a wider perspective it is helpful, by way of comparison, to juxtapose the Japanese outlook on these matters with Hindu notions about death rites and pilgrimage. Traditional India is known for its caste system, for a multitude of regional pilgrimages, and for *bhakti,* a devotional enthusiasm manifested by itinerant poets seeking literally to embody the deities they worshipped in song. Scholars agree that pilgrimage is perhaps the most prominent type of religious behavior on the Subcontinent. And much the same may be said about Japan. In Japan, however, pilgrimage networks attained a virtually national scope by the late Heian period (794–1185).[13] In contrast, Hindu pilgrimages were exceedingly various; and a survey of the practices peculiar to peregrinations in different regions would fill volumes. In other words, while it is accurate to say that pilgrimage was a pan-Indian practice, this statement ignores what pilgrimage means to people in a particular locality. As one scholar puts it,

> The pervasiveness of pilgrimage, whether in honor of a natural site, a founder figure, or a god, has prompted many to consider it a pan-Indian phenomenon; for example, [one scholar] asserts that "the sacred geography of India recognizes the whole country as a field of more than human activity. It is carried by the rivers, from the celestial region where they have their prototype and origin down to earth." When traditions of pilgrimage are taken collectively, this is an accurate impression. However,

even a brief review of the literature of pilgrimage reveals images of profound and overwhelming regionalism. In the eyes of any given pilgrim, then, all parts of India are not equal; it matters where one stands.[14]

In fact, Hindus traditionally recognize two categories of religious peregrination; one is local and the other, known as an *end-of-life* pilgrimage, is an emphatically *public* rite. Ideally,

> a Hindu should not die in his house [a private place] but on the *ghats* [steps or passage leading down to a river] of a sacred river. Even today one can find a large number of people in the pilgrim centers such as Kashi, Mathura, Vrindavan and Hardwar who come there with the intention of "getting release from their mortal bodies".... Whereas the Chinese prefer to bury their dead in their own compounds, the cremation of a Hindu in all castes takes place on a sacred *ghat,* on the banks of a river or another source of water.... Death rituals do not form an integral part of domestic rituals.[15]

In Hindu theory, rituals performed at the birth of a child, at initiation, at marriage, and for the *propitiation* of ancestors are classified as domestic rituals. In contrast, funerary rites are deemed to be *public* events; and they fall into "the same category as coronations, commemorations of victory, propitiation of gods through *soma* sacrifices, etc."[16]

The passage cited above, referring to the Chinese who "prefer to bury the dead in their own compounds," as opposed to "the cremation of Hindus of *all* castes ... on a *sacred ghat,*" helps to clarify the several ways that Hindus, Chinese, and Japanese distinguished between private matters and affairs pertaining to the public realm. Hindus regarded many things as sacred; but the sanctity ascribed to death rituals was unique. For only this type of sanctity was enjoyed by all castes. The universality of death gave funerary rites a uniquely public character. In one respect, therefore, both Hindus and the Japanese equated the term *public* with a democratized treatment of the dead. The great difference resides in the connection Hindus made between membership in a particular caste and a presumed rebirth on Earth; whereas members of the Pure Land School in Buddhist Japan looked forward to a rebirth in a heavenly paradise.

But Pure Land teachings insisted on the religious efficacy of faith. They ascribed no redemptive promise to meritorious acts. When Shinran

> …launched the Jodo Shinshu devotional Buddhist tradition in the twelfth century, he made a break with monasticism altogether, insisting that no special acts of renunciation would merit the favor of Amida Buddha and rebirth in the Pure Land. The gracious beneficence of Amida was available to all who called upon his name.[17]

Like Martin Luther's belief in the priesthood of all believers, Shinran established a radical lay orientation in Japanese Buddhism. In contrast to Jodo Shinshu, however, the vast majority of Japanese Buddhist communities have traditionally affirmed the soteriological effects of good actions. The distinction has relevance for a further and equally significant comparison, this time between Vedic culture, Japan, and China. The concept of religious merit is closely tied to *ahimsa,* a belief in the brotherhood of all sentient beings. The teaching required a renunciation of animal sacrifice. Moreover, it is noteworthy that the Chinese practiced two types of blood offerings: sacrifices to appease family ancestors and oblations to celebrate public events. Hindus also sacrificed animals at public events, as for example, at ceremonies to propitiate the gods through *soma* sacrifices. And the "propitiation of ancestors" was deemed to be a domestic ritual.[18] In this context, the term "propitiation" refers to animal sacrifice. The striking similarity with ritual sacrifices offered at ancestral tombs in China merits attention. To be sure, unlike the Chinese, Hindu offerings to family forbears were largely performed in the absence of tombs. Yet, even without a grave site, sacrifices to appease or to "propitiate" ancestors are invariably apotropaic, that is, they have powers to avert contamination, to dispel evil, and to avoid ill luck. The parallel is virtually perfect.

Summary

It is now time to review the material to be discussed in the body of the book. Definitions of identity and their relation to diction—understood here as a way or style of using words and phrases in literary traditions and in religious writings—have been a major part of the subjects discussed throughout these introductory pages. In this context the word "immanence" refers to a range of meaning, extending from the immanence in poetry describing the wordless perception of religious transcendence, to the immanence residing in relics, in spirits, in images, in sacred texts, and merely in the words pronounced in ritual. This book argues that concepts of collective and individual identity will vary according to the prevailing type of immanence. One form of immanence is related to fixed sanctity, and the other to a portable mode of sanctity. Only the latter indicates the presence of a common dead. In general, portable sanctity is dominant in high-trust societies (but see below for mention of the great exception to this, the United States). And the prevalence of widespread credence in a high-trust society contributes to the progress of social individuation. Also, a literature suggestive of a "transcendence through immanence"—as in the earlier-cited poem by a fourteenth-century Zen priest—originates largely in a culture promoting a strong sense of personal identity.

Notions of immanence and the cultural aspects of identity formation, both corporate and individual, are phenomena that vary according to the principles described above. This essay has two major subject areas. The United States, Imperial China, and several aspects of medieval and early modern Bavaria-South Germany are discussed within the theoretical framework described in the preceding pages. A concluding section deals with a multitude of religions in the ancient world. It argues that all the social and cultural factors contributing to a common dead, to cultural coherence, and to high levels of trust help to explain why Buddhism and Christianity became the first world religions.

It is noteworthy that the United States may be the only country in history which has, from the outset, enjoyed an unusually portable mode of sanctity in the absence of a common dead. A few preliminary observations help introduce the discussion of this topic in chapter 2. Protestants entering North America during the three centuries after the Reformation not only believed the Bible to be the exclusive source of sanctity, but they also assumed, and today many of them continue to assert, that biblical authority extends to the political arena. An interjection of scriptural passages into debates about public affairs incited perennial disputes between those who favored and others who opposed the conflation of biblical precepts with constitutional principles.

In some respects, the wish to politicize biblical apothegms is reminiscent of Thomas Jefferson's views about the proper form of government. To be sure, the author of the Declaration of Independence rarely cited the Bible; and he vigorously opposed governmental intrusion into religious affairs. Yet, Jefferson also largely agreed with Jean-Jacques Rousseau's affirmation that "the voice of the people is the voice of God." Although these men were inspired by very different reasons, the fact remains that Rousseau, Jefferson, and evangelical Protestants all sponsored a *speech-modeled conception of government.* Religious and political freedom were equated with "the ability to live entirely in the present."[19] This curious convergence of theologically and politically inspired rejections of the past—even though motivated by spokesmen professing contrary principles—powerfully contributed to a public repudiation of a common dead.

On this matter Jefferson was adamant. As he put it,

> It is now forty years since the constitution of Virginia was formed. The same tables inform us, that, within that period, two thirds of the adults then living are now dead. Have the remaining third, even if they had the wish, the right to hold in obedience to their will, and the laws heretofore made by them, the other two thirds, who, with themselves compose the present mass of adults? If they have not, who has? The dead? But the dead have no rights. They are nothing; and nothing cannot own Something. Where there is no substance, there can be no accident. This corporeal globe, and everything upon it, belong to the present corporeal inhabitants, during their generation.[20]

A more explicit description of a "speech-modeled conception of government" would be difficult to conceive. People living entirely in the present—amid incessant controversies about the religious or secular orientation of immediate legislation—stand as strangers to one another; and when representatives of socially isolated groups conduct public affairs, sentiments of trust are minimal.

Turn now to chapter 3. Much has been said about Imperial China. The various forms of fixed sanctity, the universality of ancestor cults, and widespread distrust—usually personified by ghosts and evil spirits—are familiar subjects requiring no further preliminary attention. Moreover, equal space has been devoted to the flip side of this state of cultural incoherence—how public funeral ceremonies, public memorials, and portable sanctity promote feelings of community, on the one hand, and strengthen the sense of personal identity among individual members of the community, on the other. Stated in more general terms, the convergence of personal and collective feelings of identity in a pre-modern society—be it in East Asia or elsewhere—takes place in the measure that socially and religiously induced feelings of individual identity have evolved in the context of a life-long and collective anticipation of religious redemption. Offered as a major hypothesis, I propose that subjective apprehension of personal identity first flourished when one or another dominant belief system traditionally encouraged the faithful to look forward to an idyllic post-mortem destiny.

This said, turn now to religious movements in which rituals are designed to create a common dead. These rites are regularly performed in the Church of Jesus Christ of Latter-day Saints (LDS), the formal name of a movement popularly called Mormonism. LDS is one of the fastest-growing religious organizations in the world. The Mormon Church in Salt Lake City—along with the Reorganized Church of Latter-Day Saints (RLDS), its headquarters in Independence, Missouri, popularly known as the Community of Christ, and other Mormon denominations—are all dedicated to establishing ritual relations between the living and the dead in every community on Earth. Rituals to *baptize* the dead inspire widespread vicarious programs, directed by Mormons, for the benefit of departed souls throughout the world.

CHAPTER 2

•◆•

Mormonism and Religious Diversity in the United States

The Nature and Significance of Biblical Readings in the History of American Mormons

Harold Bloom has long admonished against confusing the Hebrew and Christian Bibles. As he puts it,

The Hebrew Bible ought not to be confused with the Christian Bible, which is founded upon it, but which amounts to a very severe revision of the Bible of the Jews. The Jews call their Holy Scripture Tanakh, an acronym for the three parts of the Bible: Torah (the Teaching or Law, also known as the five books of Moses, or Pentateuch); Nevi'im (the Prophets); and Kethuvim (the Writings). Christians call the Hebrew Bible the Old Testament, or Covenant, in order to supersede it with their New Testament, a work that remains altogether unacceptable to Jews, who do not regard their Covenant as Old and therefore superseded. Since Christians are obliged to go on calling Tanakh an Old Testament, I myself suggest that Jewish critics and readers might speak of their Scriptures as the Original Testament, and the Christian work as the Belated Testament, for that, after all, is what it is, a revisionary work that attempts to replace a book,

Torah, with a man, Jesus of Nazareth, proclaimed as the Messiah of the House of David by Christian believers.[1]

Mormon notions of Biblical exegesis not only defy Harold Bloom's strictures, but their interpretations of Paul's letters and the First Gospel also conflict with traditional Christian views. For example, consider the Mormon renditions of two passages about baptisms on behalf of the dead. Paul's rhetorical question asks: "What do people mean by being baptized on behalf of the dead?" (1 Corinthians 15:29) In this instance Paul addresses the issue directly. A second passage refers to the same topic indirectly, and does not have the word "baptism." But it does speak to "the keys to the kingdom of Heaven" received by Peter, giving Peter "the power so to bind events on earth that they will be bound in Heaven" (Matthew 16:19). These two passages, which in fact are historically related, have a signification in Mormon theology that ignores history and also conflicts with interpretations of Christians standing outside the Mormon Church.

In Antiquity baptism was one among many different rites related to immersion in water. In pre-Christian religions baptisms were largely initiation rituals and, more importantly, many—perhaps even most of them—were thought to have purifying powers. Psychological intent largely determined the symbolic importance of any given baptismal ceremony. And some waters were reputed to have unusually efficacious cleansing properties. For example,

> Water, especially the Nile's cold water, which is believed to have regenerative powers, is used to baptize the dead in a ritual based on the Osiris myth. This ritual both assures the dead of an afterlife and rids them of blemishes that may not be taken into the other world. Baptism of the dead is also found among the Mandeans (cf. the Book of John), and a similar rite is mentionedin the Orphic tablets.[2]

Paul understood the ancient rite of baptizing the dead in terms of Jesus's resurrection. The physical body which perishes at death, explains

Paul, "is raised" as a spiritual body (I Corinthians 44). This belief has well-known Hebrew origins. A passage in 2 Maccabees, written about fifty years earlier, praises the "noble Judas" who had taken up a collection for a "sin offering" on behalf of his community's slain kinsmen, whose bodies were found with forbidden tokens representing idols. "In taking up a collection", explains the author, Judas

> acted very well and honorably, taking account of the resurrection. For if he were not expecting that those who had fallen would rise again, it would have been superfluous and foolish to pray for the dead. But if he were looking to the splendid reward that is laid up for those who fall asleep in godliness, it was a holy and pious thought (2 Mac. 44–45).

Sin offerings made to redeem the wrongdoings of slain Jewish kinsmen, so as to assure them of a resurrection, are ceremonies strikingly similar to an ancient practice that Paul described as a baptism performed "on behalf of the dead."

Turn now to the First Gospel, where Matthew explains how "the keys to the kingdom of heaven" gave Peter powers "to bind events on earth so that they will be bound in Heaven." (Matthew 16:19) In his book *Matthew's Christian-Jewish Community,* Anthony J. Saldarini explains:

> We can trace [the] uncertainty about the exact boundary between the two religions [Jewish and Christian] virtually from the emergence of the Syriac-speaking Church right down to its effective demise as a major cultural force in the Middle East [in the eighth century].[3]

According to the book of Matthew—written in Antioch in the '80s or '90s of the first century— Jewish followers of Jesus, in the Syriac-speaking Church, associated relics with the resurrection of Jesus. Only in Matthew, and not in any other Gospel, do the bodies of the saints come out of their tombs and march into Jerusalem at the moment of Jesus's resurrection (27:51–52). The difficulty in distinguishing Jewish from Christian disciples of Jesus in the Syriac-speaking Church does not, by itself, explain why both of these groups believed that buried saints rose out of their tombs and marched into Jerusalem so as to be resurrected alongside Jesus. In this passage the powers ascribed to the relics of saints were explicitly identified with Jesus's divinity. Over time, however, people worked out the implications of this passage with respect to relic veneration. At issue here are opinions about the potency of saint relics stemming from separate time periods—the view presented in Matthew at the end of the first century, and the teachings of early medieval Roman clerics.

Church spokesmen did not dispute Matthew's account of the saints who rose out of their tombs to accompany Jesus in a common resurrection. But their descriptions of phenomena believed to have ensued from the twin resurrections grew more complex over time. Reports about the rise of Jesus along with a simultaneous ascent of deceased saints from the tombs gradually acquired more and more extra-biblical detail. According to the *Oxford English Dictionary,* the phrase *odour of sanctity* refers to "a sweet or balsamic odour stated to have been exhaled by the bodies of eminent saints at their death, or on subsequent disinterment, and held to attest to their saintship." In early medieval Europe the pleasing redolence that rose from the remains of a freshly exhumed saint "proved" that the holy person, widely known for his ascetic life, had miraculously exuviated his flesh without putrefaction. About 580, Bishop Gregory of Tours, speaking very much in the spirit of Matthew's Gospel, explained that saints "never really died, since [their souls] continued to live in heaven."

The blessed effluvium emanating from the grave was a sign that the saint's soul reigned with God in paradise. In sum, "God exercises his powers through the saint at his tomb" (Bk. II, ch. 23) in much the same manner that the Lord allowed Peter "to bind events on earth so they will be bound in Heaven." The sanctified bones buried beneath the earth and the holy person's soul in heaven were, in fact, believed to be living entities, one representing a material and the other symbolizing the spiritual aspect of a venerated figure. The relics beneath the tomb and the saint's spiritual presence in heaven, when taken together, constituted a living person endowed with divine attributes. Thus, merely two centuries after the appearance of Matthew's Gospel, a sentence referring to the dualistic formula—as it is on earth so will it be in heaven—was inscribed on the tomb of St. Martin (c. 316–397) at Tours: "Here lies buried Martin the bishop of holy memory, whose soul is in the hand of God, but he is entirely here, present and manifest in all the grace of his virtues."[4]

Bearing these details in mind, one must now explain how the inscription on St. Martin's tomb is related to the doctrines, beliefs, and practices of the Church of Jesus Christ of Latter-Day Saints. The explanation begins with the extraordinary visions of Joseph Smith, who resided in New York State in the early 1800s. Joseph read the Epistle of James when he was twelve years old. At fourteen he had a religious vision. The event took place in a wood. As Joseph kneeled on the ground to pray he was enveloped by a thick darkness. After Joseph responded to this evil force by praying even more fervently, "a pillar of light" dispelled the blackness; and the Father and Son, appearing as identical figures, entered Joseph's vision. Seeking certitude about making a confessional choice, Joseph asked which religious faction he should join. The Father and Son forbade him from joining any religious sect, telling Joseph that all of them were wrong.

Ultimately, on 21 September 1823, Joseph "received three visionary visits from the angel Moroni." The angel told Joseph:

> he will be a most significant person, that a book written on gold plates will be obtained and translated and that a priesthood will be revealed to him. A "turning of hearts" of fathers and children...[will] avoid a calamity of judgment on earth.[5]

Joseph learned where the gold plates were buried; and, subsequently, he and the angel met at this site once a year, for seven consecutive years. Receiving the plates at his last meeting with the angel, Joseph rendered these writings into English, presumably with divine guidance; and they were published in *The Book of Mormon* in 1830.

Although suffering early persecution, Joseph Smith's religion became one of the most powerful in North America. Yet many people think Joseph Smith's teachings are bizarre, to say the least; and they are baffled by the astounding popularity of these teachings. There is convincing evidence to show that the hope of easy access to ritual relations with the dead, more than any other factor, explains Mormonism's success. The following passage from the final pages of Douglas Davies's book *An Introduction to Mormonism,* although written from a perspective utterly different from my own, conveys much the same message.

> In chapter 4 I have already explored death in LDS culture; here I return to the topic precisely because most Christian missions, especially in the twenty-first century, say very little about death and the afterlife: they prefer to concentrate their theological and ethical efforts on this life. Latter-Day Saints, by contrast, intensified their commitment to eternity. And in countries where Catholicism had deeply influenced popular culture, it is likely that its clear doctrinal position and its implementation through the ritual practice of temples will furnish a distinctive appeal. Christian theology at large has very little to say about death and the afterlife beyond a generalized affirmation of life after death, and in some denominations that is weak. Most formal theologies, including those of the greatest Catholic and Protestant theologians, present their briefest essays when it comes to death and heaven. Much of what they do say would have relatively little appeal to non-theologians.[6]

Both Davies and I agree, albeit for very different reasons, that "Latter-Day Saint theology is, above all else, a theology of death conquest"; and a popular yearning for membership in a trans-generational community explains why vast numbers of people in the United States and elsewhere have joined the Church of Latter-Day Saints.

Return for a moment to the angel Moroni's role in the story about the origins of *Book of Mormon.* The most striking feature is the parallel between the writings imprinted on the golden plates and the words inscribed on St. Martin's tomb. The two writings—one historical, the other theologi-cal— share the same reliquary functions. Martin's physical presence in his tomb—as distinguished from the words specifying that Martin's soul resided in the hand of God—not only worked miracles, but the powers bequeathed to his relics beneath the tomb also confirmed Martin's legal status. And the Saint's standing in Civil Law descended directly from the authority conferred on the Bishop of Rome by the relics of Peter and Paul. As Peter Brown put it, "the power of the bishop tended to coalesce with the power of the shrine."[7] According to Sir Robert Southern, "even the pope owed much of his authority to the fact that he was the guardian of Peter's bones. This brought men to Rome and made them listen to the voice of St. Peter mediated through his representation on earth."[8]

Turn now to the writings allegedly found on golden plates. Passages from the Old and New Testaments are interspersed throughout the writings proper to the *Book of Mormon*. The reader learns that Jesus made the resurrection possible by descending to Earth to atone for the sins of all mankind. Not only did Jesus atone for everyone's sin on the cross, explains Douglas Davies, "but [it is] especially in the garden of Gethsemane, where he takes the sins of the world upon himself and bleeds in every pore. The outcome…is the unconditional benefit of the resurrection." This gospel message

> must be heard and accepted and result in baptism and confirmation at the hands of the Melchizedek-priesthood of the Church.[9]

In sum, the divine grace emanating from Jesus's atonement allows for a baptism of the dead and, ultimately, at a future date, for the resurrection of every person on Earth.

Moreover, the Melchizedek-priesthood's authority to baptize the dead is closely related to Mormon pilgrimage practices. Few pilgrimage shrines are located in the United States. Mormon enthusiasm for religious peregrination—a rare phenomenon in the United States—comes from the acceptance of a purported first-century teaching that Jesus was, in fact, "a Melchizedek redivivus." In Genesis (13:17) God tells Abram to "walk through the length of the land, for I will give it to you." Abram's armies ultimately conquer the land. After defeating the last enemy forces, the

> king of Sodom went out to meet [Abram] at the valley of Shaveh (the King's Valley). And Melchizedek king of Salem brought out bread and wine; he was the priest of God most

High. And he blessed him and said, "Blessed be Abram by God most High maker of heaven and earth; and blessed be God most High who has delivered your enemies into your hand!"

An apocalyptic text, entitled *Melchizedek,* a Christian writing, has Melchizedek, the "priest of God" transmit communications he received from God to an unidentified spiritual elite. The revelatory messages concern the relationship between Jesus and Melchizedek. Some revelations transport Melchizedek into the future. In one instance, when he is projected forward in time, Melchizedek appears as "the crucified, resurrected, and triumphant savior himself." The text "teaches the identity of Jesus Christ with Melchizedek," a view which, in turn, was probably derived from an interpretation of a verse from the book of Hebrews (7:3):[10]

He [Melchizedek] is without father or mother or genealogy, and he has neither a beginning of days nor an end of life, but resembling the Son of God he continues as priest forever.

In March 1829, Robert Southey made a remarkable prophecy with regard to religious events in North America:

America is in more danger from religious fanaticism. The Government there not thinking it necessary to provide religious instruction for the people in any of the New States, the prevalence of superstition, and that, perhaps, in some wild and terrible shape, may be looked for as one likely consequence of this great and portentous omission. An Old Man of the Mountain might find dupes and followers as readily as the All-friend Jemima; and the next Aaron Burr who seeks to carve a kingdom for himself out of the overgrown territories of the Union may discern that fanaticism is the most effective weapon with which ambition can arm itself; that the way for both is prepared by that immorality which the want of religion naturally and necessarily induces, and that Camp Meetings may be very well directed to forward the designs of Military Prophets. Were there another Mohammed to arise, there is no part of the world where he would find more scope or fairer opportunity than in that part of the Anglo-American Union into which the older States continually discharge the restless part of their population, leaving Laws and Gospel to overtake it if they can, for in the march of modern colonization both are left behind.[11]

Mormon Pilgrimage

The pilgrimage practices sponsored by the Melchizedek priesthood in the Church of Latter-Day Saints are inspired by readings from ancient religious documents. As we saw, God's high priest, Melchizedek, blesses Abram for having carried out Yahweh's command to "walk through the length of the land" that the Lord promised to bestow on His people. The legitimacy of pilgrimage, however, says nothing about the styles and occasions of pilgrimage nor about the locations and the architecture of holy shrines, not to mention instructions concerning the dedication of these sites. Since Melchizedek, God's high priest, was identified with Jesus Christ, the Melchizedek priesthood did not countenance saint shrines—a decision made somewhat incongruous by the fact that "Mormonism" is a popular term for the Church of Latter-Day Saints. Fortunately, historical models of shrines dedicated to Christ were legion. Those considered most appropriate—that is, sites thought to be illustrative of a Mormon history seen from a theological perspective—were pilgrimage places built as "pious simulations" of the *via cruces* to Mount Calvary, situated largely in Italy, Spain, Portugal, Germany, and Brazil. Pilgrims intent on ascending to a simulacrum of Mount Calvary could witness multi-media exhibitions of Jesus's Passion without having to make the perilous and expensive journey to Jerusalem.[12]

Today a similar phenomenon may be observed in Atlantic City, Wyoming. Teenagers clad in nineteenth-century pioneer outfits pull unwieldy handcarts over rocky terrain, reenacting a historic Mormon pilgrimage in 1856. At that time, more than 200 half-starved Mormon converts from Europe—pushing and pulling handcarts—died in a fierce autumn blizzard as they attempted to reach the Mormon Zion, Salt Lake City.[13] In art-historical parlance, explains Mitchell Merback, Calvary, meaning "a place of skulls," denotes "a type of elaborated or 'historiated' Crucifixion, set into a land-scape with an expanded, often quite dense cast of characters."[14] Similarly, a public memorial to a dark chapter in Mormon history has now become a booming spiritual enterprise, reenacted both on the original route and also by Mormon communities as distant as Cambodia and Sierra Leone. The European and Brazilian shrines, simulating the Passion at Calvary, remind us that the memory of the handcart trek is becoming for *twelve million* Mormons today what the memory of the Exodus from Egypt is to Jews and the "heigira" from Mecca is to Muslims. Moreover, the sheer multitude of Mormons, perhaps more than any other factor, may account for the immense popularity of Mel Gibson's film *The Passion of Christ*.

Religious Diversity, Protestant Militancy, and Political Divisions

Aspirations to reside in a land enjoying religious liberty motivated many Europeans to depart for North America in the seventeenth and eighteenth centuries. After the Declaration of Independence, the constitutional pro-visions providing for both the nonestablishment of religion and also for the protection of the "free exercise" of religion have permitted the United States to become the most religiously diverse nation on Earth. In a mar-velous book, Diana L. Eck has traced in great detail both the influence of America on non-Christian religions and the influence of Buddhist, Muslim, Hindu, Sikh, Jain, and Zoroastrian communities, to name only a few, on Christian communities in the United States.[15] Interfaith ten-sions are widespread, and often most intense in smaller communities. For example, the problems raised by the practice of animal sacrifice by members of the Santeria Church of the Lukumi Babalu Aye in Hialeah, Florida, have potentially far-reaching implications. An estimated

> fifty thousand practitioners of the Afro-Caribbean Santeria religion now live in South Florida, and their ceremonial life

includes the sacrifice of chickens, pigeons, or other small animals to the *orisha,* their gods.

Outraged by Santeria's ritual oblations, "the city council of Hialeah passed three ambiguous ordinances that worked effectively to prohibit animal sacrifice within the city limits." In response, officials of the Santeria community complained that the ordinances "did not prohibit the killing of animals within city limits for secular reasons but only for religious ones and only, seemingly, for those of the Santeria religion. Indeed, the ordinances specifically excluded Jewish kosher slaughter practices." Some citizens, inspired by more tolerant sentiments, quipped that "Babalu Aye was being persecuted for killing a few chickens with a prayer," while local poultry companies, such as Colonel Sanders and Frank Perdue, "kill tens of thousands" of chickens without a single prayer. Litigation about these issues continued up to the United States Supreme Court, which finally ruled in favor of the Church of Lukumi Babalu Aye. As Justice Anthony M. Kennedy wrote:

> Although the practice of animal sacrifice may seem abhorrent to some, religious beliefs need not be acceptable, logical, consistent, or comprehensible to others in order to merit First Amendment protection.[16]

The enmity and bitterness engendered by years of costly litigation were by no means limited to the city of Hialeah. Social tensions have ramified throughout the region where Santeria religion is practiced. Also, speeches from public officials, orations from church ministers, and widespread news commentaries have elevated disputes concerning periodic ritual sacrifices of a few chickens and pigeons in Hialeah to the level of serious ideological division in many South Florida communities.

Evangelicals, Fundamentalists, and other militant Protestant groups exemplify a mentality prepared to make a public issue out of practices, however trifling, that are deemed to be contrary to their convictions. At issue here is the distinction between an order and a sect. An order is "a community of specialized professionals within a larger religious body, while the sect breaks with that body to form its own doctrine, clergy, and thoroughly distinct lay following *(secta)*."[17] To count the number of Protestant sects in the United States today would require months of research. And the rise of Protestant sectarianism is of a piece with a religious militancy that threatens to transform the principle of religious liberty into an instrument for establishing laws hostile to the functions of a civil society.

Historically, the ideal of religious freedom is associated with evolution of the concept of a *public opinion* in Western Europe and in North America during the mid and later eighteenth century. For an opinion to become *public* it must be perceived as a collective or widely espoused view—features that overlap with super-societal traits that George Lakoff calls *values*. Applying cognitive sciences to contemporary politics, Lakoff shows that values are most often thought to originate in realms beyond personal experience. Standards believed to stand above daily affairs influence our behavior to a degree roughly commensurate with the emotions we invest in these criteria. Deep attachment to a paramount source of personal experience may promote civic and even religious division—as in contemporary controversies about the *political* precepts of evangelical spokesmen. Yet, in some measure, these very convictions may also be an essential aspect of *both* collective *and* personal identity.[18] An Evangelical and an atheist, for example, might work together to file an official complaint against a corrupt bureaucrat.

This said, return now to the eighteenth-century principle that an opinion becomes *public* when it is perceived as a collective or widely espoused point of view. Today *public opinion* is usually measured (and also partially created) by responses to questions presented by polling organizations. Published responses to these questions keep readers informed of currently held common convictions. Seen from this perspective, the term *public opinion* refers to a general condition of social awareness, that is, a collective state of mind. Since people have been more or less aware of the existence of a popular mind-set since at least the nineteenth century, the rise of *public opinion* may well be a chief source of the character traits portrayed in a personified figure of a nation—such as John Bull or Uncle Sam, symbolic personages presently called organological analogies. Although the emotive and cultural features are emblematic, the images show a clear sense of self.[19]

The sense of membership symbolized by an organological analogy has led some scholars to see it as a symbol of modern civil society. If the adjective *civil* refers to *non*-institutionalized and *voluntary* social movements then, and only then, may an organological analogy symbolize a civil society. At issue here is the social concept of embodiment. In the Middle Ages people often ascribed religious and supernatural attributes to kings and other exalted personages—figures who were thought to embody the political and religious structures they represented. Some monarchs literally personified the societies they represented, heralding, as it were, the emblematic representations of a personified nation in the eighteenth century. Previously, embodiment was thought to be an involuntary state. In contrast, according to the enlightened elite in the eighteenth century, *conversation* was both a disembodied condition and an ideal instrument of socialization. The view that conversation is at once a "civilizing" and also a voluntary activity was central to the concept of a "civil society" among "enlightened" Europeans in the eighteenth century.

Beginning in the late seventeenth century, educated Englishmen and Frenchmen frequented coffee shops, read newspapers, and discussed public affairs. They also gathered regularly in public places, private homes, and salons to discuss theater, politics, and current affairs. Individuals often met one another for the first time at one of these public gatherings. The frequency of these common encounters strengthened the tendency to refer to all participants in these activities as members of *a public voice.* In sum, the expression "public voice"—a locution ultimately giving rise to the concept of a "public opinion"— referred to the disembodied and, therefore, purified emanations of enlightened conversation. A common desire for civic and social improvement, and the belief that reason and good-will are the most effective instruments toward this end, often made religion an object of contempt and satire. Claude Adrien Helvetius (1715–1771) managed to articulate these views in two very brief assertions:

What makes men happy is liking what they have to do. This is a principle on which society is not founded.

We don't call a man mad who believes he eats God [the Eucharist], but we do the one who says he is Jesus Christ.[20]

Movements to further the growth of "civil society" in North America began before the Revolution against English rule, and largely within Protestant traditions. As we saw, however, after the Revolution Protestant movements proved to be hostile to the concept of a civil society. More precisely, largely secular and even irreligious movements in support of a civil society appear at different times on the two continents. In Europe, Luther's belief in the priesthood of all believers—a doctrine curiously parallel to Shinran's teaching promising rebirth in the Pure Land to all who called upon the name of Amitabha, the Buddha of infinite light, in twelfth-century Japan—initially cut across any notion of a civil society. Western European elites began to divest themselves of this impediment by the late seventeenth century. And in North America people such as Benjamin Franklin and Thomas Jefferson were heirs to a tradition known as "Civil Tongues" and "Polite Letters" in British America.[21] A massive growth in Protestant immigration and the divisions created by the Civil War sharply limited the influence of innumerable representatives of civil society such as Emerson, Thoreau, and Walt Whitman.

CHAPTER 3

•◆•

Relics, Dreams, and Theater:
Ancestor Cults and the Rise of World Religions

An Introductory Excursus

BELIEFS ABOUT DEATH, DEFILEMENT, and the afterlife have been discussed in connection with fixed and portable modes of sanctity. These phenomena will now be presented in a much wider perspective. Since the end of World War II, basic terms such as *culture, state,* and *religion* have new and often uncertain usages. For example, the equivocality pertaining to the word *state* resides in the fact that "a state exists chiefly in the hearts and minds of its people. If they do not believe it," explains a distinguished medievalist, "no logical exercise will bring it to life."

> A human community must persist in space and time if it is to become a state. Only by living and working together *in a given area for many generations* can a group of people develop the patterns of organization which are essential for state-building. [italics added][1]

To say that a state exists only (i) "in the hearts and minds of its people," who (ii) lived and worked "together in a particular area for many generations" tells us that popular rituals recognizing the living presence of departed souls would eventually have the effect of ascribing a collective identity to a people who had lived and died in earlier times. In the course of centuries mortuary and memorial rites will, at some point, convey a backward projection sufficiently powerful to give a human community remote retroactive origins. An acknowledgement of a collective identity extending many centuries into the past not only allowed officials to establish political sovereignty in the present; but a sovereignty originating in a distant past also possessed a power continuing indefinitely in time. Thus, by conferring a retrospective identity to earlier generations, authorities created a contemporary corporate entity possessing immortal qualities believed to be inherent in a power recognized to have no temporal limits.

Seen from a cross-cultural perspective, therefore, establishment of political sovereignty was inseparable from processes whereby ordinary people participated in the immortal attributes ascribed to kings and other exalted figures personifying a sovereign power. A subjective sense of personal identity generally varied according to the greater or lesser distribution of the immortal qualities believed to proceed from the offices of a sovereign government. In some countries ordinary people assumed they participated or shared in the immortal qualities they ascribed to their sovereigns. And the contrary was true for other societies. The participatory elements inherent to the concept of sovereignty were unstable; and they were also unequally distributed among different peoples, both in antiquity and throughout the Middle Ages.

Notions of Kingship and Immortality in Imperial China and Japan

The imperial Chinese state begins with the Qui dynasty's "First Emperor" or Shihuangdi, the person who unified all the Chinese states in 221 BCE. Fifteen years later the Han dynasty (206 BCE–220 CE) made the Mandate of Heaven *(Tian ming)* the only theoretical principle justifying an imperial rule. As a famous scholar puts it,

> the ancient idea of a heavenly or cosmic mandate to rule was the only theoretical verification of legitimacy that traditional

Chinese political thinkers and dynastic founders ever agreed upon. To claim that validating mandate demanded more than the power to conquer or coerce. A new aspirant to legitimate rule, besides displaying raw military power sufficient to suppress all opposition and thereby unify the realm, also had to make plausible his claim that heaven had transferred the Mandate to himself and to his lineage (his dynasty), and that he had met convincingly the *ritual* requirements of universal rulership [italics added].[2]

From Han times onward "the notion that a legitimate new dynasty should be discontinuous with its predecessor" (even though its Mandate was usually transmitted through that predecessor) continued down to the end of the Qing in 1911.[3]

The discontinuity in royal succession entailed by the Mandate from Heaven effectively eliminated participatory elements from the Chinese concept of sovereign authority. No explicit doctrine distinguished power from authority; and rituals proved to be the chief, often even the only way to ascribe legitimacy to the policies and actions of royal as well as local officials. To ritualize all processes of government in the name of a Mandate from Heaven was also to divorce ritual from religious belief. The persistence of ancestor worship and an ensuing recourse to ritual in most aspects of private life—in virtually every sphere and at all levels of government—effectively excluded ancestor veneration from ritual life in the public sphere. Ritual defined almost every aspect of private and public life. As mentioned earlier, the ubiquity of ancestor veneration severely restricted the exercise of trans-kin authority in the public sphere. To cite again from Professor Mote's work:

> The emperor was ritual head of the state, analogous to the head of every Chinese clan or lineage, by which every person in society was bound to a surname and to family responsibilities. As the head of the imperial clan, he thus was a model for the maintenance of the *atomized* family-based ancestor veneration that *held priority among all forms of religion in society.* And

the emperor was held to *embody* and to have responsibility for upholding all the values of the society. But he was *not expected to assume such responsibilities in an open, public manner. He did not interact personally with any sector of society, and did not play a significant political role in public life* [italics added].[4]

The contrast with the exercise of royal authority in Japan is immense. As mentioned earlier, when Japanese kings retired as monks in the Heian period (794–1185), they sponsored the bestowal of Buddhist names upon ordinary people at death, contributing thereby to the religious redemption of all their subjects. In medieval Japan *everyone* participated in the immortal attributes ascribed to rulers of a sovereign state. Conversely, the Chinese emperor was: (1) "a model for the maintenance of the *atomized* family-based ancestor veneration *that held priority among all forms of religion in society*"; (2) although the emperor was held "to *embody* and to have responsibility for upholding all the values of society," the Chinese emperor, unlike his Japanese counterpart, "did *not* interact personally with any sector of society." Thus, in principle ordinary people in China *NEVER* participated in the immortal attributes ascribed to rulers of a sovereign state.

Ancestor Cults in Small- and Large-Scale Societies: A Cross-Cultural Perspective

Among the social consequences of death, one in particular seems to be truly universal: emotional bonds continue to bind the survivors to a deceased long after his or her demise. Although the person disappears, relations with the defunct persist. The experience is pan-human; and people everywhere adopt measures—traditionally called acts of *separation* and severance—to terminate close contacts with the recent dead. This type of practice varies widely across cultures. In small, face-to-face societies the survivors constitute the entire community. Everyone is affected directly by an individual's demise because everyone knows the person who died. The survivors tend to respond in unison when personal attachments to the deceased are

shared by the entire community. Typically, a tribe, clan, or village per-
forms rituals to "kill" the dead person. By slaying the defunct in absentia,
as it were, people periodically sever their bonds to the deceased in the
course of a series of funerary and mortuary rites—the rites of separation
and severance mentioned above—held at specified occasions throughout
an interval which varies cross-culturally from a few weeks to several years.
Ultimately, at the time of severance, the deceased loses his or her name,
vanishing forever from ritual memory.

From an observer's point of view ceremonial erasure of the name constitutes oblivion. To the participants, however, a ritually imposed anonymity
marks the moment when the deceased descends beneath the earth to join
a formless, undifferentiated community of ancestors—usually known as
a "common dead." In a small-scale society, where rites of separation and
severance are performed in unison, the term "common dead" refers to
the orchestration of mourning. For only a common mourner can mourn
a common dead. Proper execution of communal obsequies establishes a
collective identity, a coexistence that is perceived to be a social body or
corpus encompassing *both* the living *and* the departed members of the
community.

In this context, ancestors appear as a post-severance generation. And
entry into this age-group is seen as a form of transport. Death functions as
a vehicle, carrying village, tribal, and clan dead to lower levels of a cosmos
imagined to be beneath the earth. In face-to-face societies netherworlds
function as mirror images of communities from which all inhabitants are
destined to descend after their demise. Here the word "descend," used
both as a verb and a noun, refers to: (i) a temporal or generational line
of descent; (ii) a physiological decline or decurrence, a "running down,"
in sum, a diminished level of life-activity; (iii) an actual journey, a downward passage into regions beneath the earth. With respect to ancestors,
therefore, the term *descend* designates a state of collective being; the word
also refers to a subterranean territory having dimensions commensurate
with the boundaries defining the size of the lands occupied by the living.

In sum, to have the dead join with the living in the conduct of daily affairs
imparts a material continuity to the corporate existence of a face-to-face

community. Belief in the post-mortem continuity of a *corporeal* existence provides the trans-generational impetus required for the social corpus—usually a village, tribe, or clan of about two hundred people or less—to be greater than the mere numerical sum of its living members. *To attain a somatic union with the dead has been a chief purpose of ancestor cults in large- and small-scale societies throughout human history.* Why do ancestor cults everywhere seek a somatic union with the dead? The reason resides in the distinction between the identity of an individual and the identity ascribed to a collectivity. The term "ancestor" refers to a deceased family member whose post-mortem identity, residing in the family name, disappears with the loss of the name; and the name will live as long as the ancestor continues to be fed. Food offerings allow an ancestor's corporeal longevity to be much longer than the life-span of people living on Earth. But blood sacrifices also set temporal limits to the ritual retention of an ancestor's name. For at some point the name disappears from ritual existence.

Feeding Ancestors and Feeding Gods

Individuals who feed ancestors look forward to membership in a post-mortem community virtually identical to the one they leave at their demise. But blood sacrifices offered to ancestors beneath the earth also presuppose the eventual demise of individual ancestors. Conversely, in the ancient Mediterranean where animal sacrifices were offered to gods in the sky, people believed that many of these deities were immortal. According to ancient Greco-Roman traditions, some gods were described as "eternals," while others were called "immortals." Sky gods like Zeus and Apollo were eternals; they escaped the processes of birth and death. In contrast, immortals, once human beings, were erstwhile kings and heroes who ascended to heaven because of their benefactions to mankind. These individuals had to die before attaining immortality. Admission to heaven also presupposed an out-of-body existence in a realm very different from the society the deceased knew on Earth. Contrary to these views, Christians believed in a bodily resurrection. Yet, despite the differences separating those who affirmed from others who denied the bodily nature of an afterlife, both pagans and Christians imagined heaven to be a totally user-friendly environment located somewhere in the sky.

Pagan notions of immortality were of course more ancient than Christian doctrines of eternal life. In ancient Greece, for example, some people equated immortality with a cultural transformation of the dead as early as the fifth century BCE. Scholars are unanimous in this matter:

> What is not in dispute is that the belief in the underworld did not go entirely unchallenged in the Classical period and that a new idea grew up, probably in the first half of the fifth century, of the *psychai* [souls] of the dead being transported to heaven.[5]

The concept of a post-mortem world located somewhere in the sky, bereft of specific cultural continuity, is a thought utterly contrary to the presuppositions governing ancestor cults. First of all, ancestors don't die. They merely cease to exist at the time of severance, the moment when they lose their names and vanish from ritual memory. In some cases ancestors are ritually destroyed before traditional rites of severance. Even collective extermination of the *post*-severance or *common* dead was not an unusual procedure.

The Jewish God, for example, resorted to mass exhumations in order to annihilate the forbears of *all* the residents of ancient Jerusalem. Speaking through the mouth of his prophet, Jeremiah, the Lord threatened the common dead of Jerusalem with mass oblivion:

> The bones of the kings of Judah, the bones of its princes, the bones of the priests, the bones of the prophets, and the bones of the inhabitants of Jerusalem shall be brought out of their tombs; and they shall be spread before the sun and the moon and all the host of heaven.... They shall not be gathered or buried; they shall be as dung on the surface of the ground. (Jeremiah 8:1–3)

To dig up and disperse someone's bones was to obliterate his or her post-memorial or post-severance name. In ancient Palestine names were forever interred with the remains of the dead at a secondary burial. About eight months after an initial burial the corpse was exhumed; the last pieces of flesh were removed from the bones, and a subsequent re-interment in a family or communal ossuary constituted severance. The name of the deceased was ritually buried with the final disposal of his or her "dry bones," a biblical term referring to bones ritually prepared for second-ary burial (e.g. Ezekiel 37:10). In the Near East and Mesopotamia, ritual execution of the dead also functioned as an instrument of warfare. Exhu-mation and dispersion of the bones of an entire royal dynasty, for exam-ple, afflicted the society with an immediate threat of cultural extinction. For example, around 645 BCE, about two generations before Jeremiah's prophecy in Jerusalem, the Assyrian monarch Ashurbanipal described the vengeance he had wreaked on the "traitorous" Elamites:

> I have pulled down and destroyed the tombs of their earlier *and* later kings ... and I exposed them to the sun. I took away their bones to Assyria. I put restlessness on their *ghosts,* I deprived them of *food offerings* and libations of water [italics added].[6]

Abduction of the dynastic bones transformed the remains of Elamite kings into ghosts. And it was the ghosts, not the dynastic bones, who were deported to Assyria, no doubt as prisoners of war. A desecration and dep-redation of royal tombs turned royal ancestors into homeless specters; and the ensuing vagabondage deprived them of sustenance. The punishment inflicted on the phantoms of former Elamite monarchs reminds us that alleged maltreatment of ancestors also "put restlessness on the ghosts" and demons that haunted the people of Imperial China.

Ascribing Names: *The Named and the Nameless Dead*

Ancestors are venerated in societies where laws of inheritance and rules per-taining to social stratification continue to be enforced in a post-mortem population. The nameless dead (the deceased who no longer receive food offerings) stand outside the communities of ancestors, and are gener-ally thought to be "hungry ghosts"—erstwhile ancestors who, deprived of the offerings necessary to retain their names, were transformed into nameless and noxious spirits. Hungry ghosts are ancestors who suffered a *ritual* death. In contrast, holy persons perceived to have suffered a *social* death remain very much alive. The Buddha and his followers, much like Jesus and his disciples five hundred years later, were itinerant ascetics. An ascetic who followed either Sakyamuni or Jesus was "a man who had made himself 'dead.' But the death was a *social* death, and did not follow from a mortification of the body" (italics added).[7] In contrast, deceased family members kept ritually alive with food offerings, known as ancestors, are beings believed to embody kinship norms governing the laws of family, royal, and even priestly succession.

Hungry ghosts personify the putrefaction and ritual contagion issuing from untended corpses. Or, when viewed from another perspective, the decomposition of unburied corpses symbolized an impending dissolution of both the laws of inheritance and the rules for social stratification believed to be embodied by ancestors in societies where their cults were dominant. A single line from the New Testament testifies to the pervasive fear of the noxious emanations from burial places, imagined to be especially virulent when they proceeded from forgotten grave sites. In the Gospel of Luke, the author has Jesus declare: "Woe to you [Pharisees]! For you are like graves which are not seen, and men walk over them without knowing it" (11:44). Matthew's Jesus fulminates against his enemies: "Woe to you, scribes and hypocrites! for you are like white-washed tombs, which outwardly appear beautiful, but within they are full of dead men's bones and all uncleanness" (23:27).

The complaints ascribed to Jesus in the gospels of Luke and Matthew were denunciations directed against age-old mortuary practices. Throughout the ancient Mediterranean—as in China and every other large-scale society with powerful ancestor cults—people believed that ritual food and sepultures not only kept the dead permanently entombed, but that these ossuaries also contributed to the comfort and physical preservation of the deceased. Anchoring erstwhile members of a blood-line in their tombs also served to designate the area of jurisdiction controlled by the living members of a particular lineage.

Although these phenomena were historically cross-cultural and are presently well known to scholars, their implications with regard to "immortals" in Imperial China sometimes escape learned attention. Immortals, also called transcendents, were thought to be individuals who never died. Their corporeal persistence through time signified a cultural stasis—a socially shared representation of an *embodied* socio-cultural continuity remaining eternally unchanged. A belief that imperishable bodies represent cultural immutability seems to reflect pre-imperial religious traditions. Two sources of opposition to these beliefs followed from the establishment of the Han Empire. First, literati tenets and Confucian teachings promoted ritual regulations that encompassed the entire society, extending from the King to the lower social orders—a universalism contrary to local teachings and practices. Second, Buddhist monks, being ascetics who rejected animal sacrifices in the name of a cult founded outside of China, threatened the pre-imperial and age-old right of local practitioners to mediate relations between the living and the dead. In response to this "foreign" threat to parochial ritual supremacy in funerary matters, a newly formed Taoist movement—led by a "Celestial Master" and his subordinate priests, beginning around 150 CE—launched an organized campaign to reject animal sacrifice so as to ensure the celestial preservation of the human person. These practices allowed Chinese immortals, believed to be transcendent personages, to stay eternally Chinese. Ritual preservation of an earthly body in heaven was, so to speak, the obverse of ritual offerings to preserve embodied ancestors in the netherworld.

Chinese immortals bring to mind the extraordinary longevity ascribed to Methuselah, Noah, Abraham, and other Old Testament worthies reputed to have lived before the Flood. The agelessness and enduring physicality ascribed to these figures represent a belief in the unalterable continuity of indigenous traditions throughout time. In this respect, their agelessness resembles the somatic continuity enjoyed by three types of Chinese supernatural figures: the immortals, the gods, and ancestors. Just as the Old Testament worthies were well nourished and retained their ageless physicality, so the Chinese transcendents, refusing only meat, called "blood food," accepted food offerings, if they were freely given and vegetarian.

In contrast, gods and ancestors usually required blood sacrifices offered at fixed locations. The unrestrained mobility enjoyed by immortals in the Chinese skies removed all elements of coercion from their cult. Had Chinese immortals remained earth-bound, they would have lost their immortality and been forever confined to their tombs. Obligation and blood offerings at a fixed location signify the somatic continuity ascribed to ancestors. Compare for a moment two opposing ideals of cultural fixity: the cultural stasis represented by mobile air-borne Chinese immortals as opposed to the cultural immutability and corporeal agelessness enjoyed by ancient Egyptian mummies. However various, the three representations of immortality—Chinese immortals, Old Testament worthies prior to the Flood, and Egyptian mummies—testify to cross-cultural efforts to make a ritual preservation of the human body an essential feature of a timeless *cultural* continuance. The division separating purified beings in the sky and polluted spirits on earth—a contrast between one type of continuity (above the navel) and a different form of continuity (below the navel)—represents an effort to distinguish between ideals related to a personal destiny as opposed to rituals designed to ensure a corporate persistence in time. In sum, two forms of identity are at issue. On the one hand, consider the immortals. The corporeal imperishability they enjoyed points to an individual, not to a corporate destiny. On the other hand, cults to local gods and ancestors flourished within a collective framework of competing lineages.

According to Kristofer Schiffer, the immortals

> are just the opposite of the gods of the people, whose temples *(miao)* are in many respects funerary monuments. Indeed, the point of origin of their worship is often a tomb or mausoleum of the saint or deity. The first temple built to Ma-tsu, in her native village on the island of Mei-chou, used to hold the relic of her mummified body.... The men who killed Lord Kuan built him a tomb, which became the first place of worship.

> *The gods are linked to particular places and ... their cults define communities in political and administrative terms. Moreover, the gods of the people are often considered collective ancestors* [italics added].[8]

"Collective ancestors" constitute a common dead who are confined to a locality. Like their counterparts in ancient Palestine, the communities of common dead in China were also subject to mass executions. For example, when emperors found local gods troublesome, they exterminated the offending deities by ritually removing their names from official lists of approved cults. To "kill" local gods, to withdraw a provincial population's right to invoke their presence, was to destroy the common dead whom these deities had represented. Animal sacrifices to regional gods also fed the collective ancestors with whom they were identified. Supernatural beings who consume the same blood-food—even if they represent a separate category of being—participate in a common carnivorous nature. This is why Chinese gods are not clearly distinguishable from ancestors.

Food Offerings and Geomancy in China

Ordinary death-day sacrifices placed before tablets in the lineage hall or on a domestic altar have traditionally been largely the same as the common fare of villagers. Prior to eating a meal, a family and its guests would present the various dishes to the family ancestors. In contrast, sacrifices offered at graves are dry and unpalatable. Supernatural beings receive different fare. They are

> offered food that is less transformed, and therefore less like human food.... Of all the supernaturals, ancestors are probably the most like those who offer them food. As ancestors in halls or domestic shrines they are well-known kinsmen with distinctive, individual identities; they can be spoken to, apologized to, thanked and so on.
>
> The gods on a more distant level receive offerings according to their rank.... The difference between Tho-te-kong, the

earth god, … and ancestors … is like the difference between a kinsman and a local policeman … [a figure less well known, less trusted, less accessible].

Moving to the top of the hierarchy, the highest god, Thi-kong, receives the most untransformed food … raw fowl with a few tail feathers left unplucked and entrails hanging about their necks; a whole raw pig with its entrails hanging about its neck [etc].[9]

A similar principle of proximity and distance may apply to food offerings to Chinese immortals. Since transcendents transformed their own food by alchemical means, one might suppose that they received untransformed food offerings. At any rate, we do know that the Chinese offered uncooked, that is, untransformed rice, to ghosts, on the one hand, and presented only cooked rice to ancestors, on the other. Moreover, the symmetry may be taken a step further. The alchemical learning required to preserve bodies indefinitely has a parallel in the knowledge necessary for practicing grave geomancy.

Taoist alchemy changed basic elements—such as rock crystals—into a body preservative that could be ingested naturally, like ordinary food. A pseudoscience called geomancy tells a practitioner how to find favorable places to dig a grave (among many other things, such as the placement and construction of buildings). At an ideal location the forces of the earth are at once favorable to the comfort of the dead and contribute to the worldly prosperity of their descendants. The skills required for an expert selection of a burial site included, for example, making the size and depth of a grave correspond to the requirements ascribed to its location so as to work out the proper arrangement of the grave goods. By the tenth century "belief in the geomancy of graves pervaded all levels" of Chinese society. Elites and literati "went to great efforts to find old graves, others to preserve graves … [and] to assure the continuance of rites.[10] In sum, alchemy maintained the integrity of bodies in the sky, while geomancy and restoration of old graves—along with inexhaustible supplies of ritual food—assured both the long-term and psychological well-being of buried ancestors.

The relation between food offerings to supernatural beings and the imperial destruction of local gods, on the one hand, and a corresponding annihilation of the common dead in the regions of the erstwhile deities, on the other, needs to be defined. As mentioned earlier, an emperor's ability to exterminate gods who represented ancestors and the popular identification of local gods with collective ancestors indicates that both gods and ancestors may be sources of corpse defilement. Conversely, the *voluntary* character of food offerings to Chinese transcendents guaranteed their purity. Two reasons explain why no defilement proceeded from a personal contact with an immortal. First, Chinese immortals never died; and, secondly, imperishable bodies do not decompose. No putrefaction takes place in the sky. And the absence of corrupting influences emanating from celestial beings—and the corresponding purity ascribed to immortals—explains why contact with a transcendental had invariably beneficial effects. However, since immortals can be defiled from contact with humans, people ritually purified themselves in expectation of such encounters. All these ritual classifications—beneficence proceeding from both self-purification and abstention from blood-offerings and an assimilation of corpse defilement with animal sacrifice—point to complex patterns of linked binary opposites having a broad cross-cultural validity.

Immortals and Historical Stages in Chinese Concepts of Kingship[11]

Sinologists think Mencius's (c. 382–300 BCE) discussion of the Mandate of Heaven *(tian ming)* to be the standard account of the early concept of political succession between dynasties. The king, called Son of Heaven *(tianzi),* acted as the primary interlocutor between Heaven and Earth. This role may go back considerably before Mencius (the date seems to be uncertain). When he acted in this capacity, the King mediated relationships between gods and men and between the living and the dead. In the course of time many of these religious functions devolved upon other officials at the court. Moreover, shamans also mediated between gods and men and between the living and the dead. With the expansion of the Chinese State—accompanied by a corresponding gradual downward expansion of the imperial paradigm of the King as the Son of Heaven, extending throughout Chinese society—conflicts arose between the old kingly prerogatives, and state officials, and these local shamans. Eventually many different players competed for the role of mediator between the human and non-human realms: officials at court, local shamans, Taoist priests, Buddhist monks, and where family sacrifices were concerned, the male head of the household.

The myth of a goddess called the "Queen Mother of the West" may be understood in the context of these disputes. Works dating from the later second century CE show the goddess seated on a throne atop of Mount Kunlun in western China. After the turn of the millennium, in the later Han Dynasty (206 BCE–220 CE),

> Heaven possessed purpose, will, and intelligence, and expressed its judgments in tangible signs.... During the Han people were engaged in the search for immortality.... The Queen Mother ... became the focus of appeals for longevity.... She gained the ability to help people in their everyday life and even the power to rescue people from hell on earth. In this new form ... the Queen Mother became a transcendent deity and a religious idol.

Like the Buddha Maitreya, "the Queen Mother was seen as a messianic figure: she or her messenger would descend to this world to save her followers and bring justice."[12]

Buddhist influences, which were strong in the third century CE, may account for the popular ascription of quasi-redemptive powers to the Queen Mother of the West. Especially noteworthy is the Buddhist story of Mu-lien, which enjoyed a much greater popularity beginning in the late third century CE. This tale describes (i) the punishment of a cruel and evil-doing widow, Chi'ng-ti, who died and fell into the Avici hell, the Hell of "No-interval"; and (ii) how her son Mu-lien, a Buddhist monk endowed with supernatural powers, descended into the netherworld and found his mother in the deepest hell, suffering from hunger. (iii) Unable to feed his mother because all the food he gave her changed into fire or salt water in front of her mouth, Mu-lien asked the Buddha Sakyamuni for help. (iv) With the Buddha's aid, Mu-lien saved his mother through the ritual offering of the "yu-lan-p'en," on the fifteenth day of the seventh month, the end of the summer retreat for the *sangha* (the monastery).[13] Unlike traditional offerings to ancestors, Mu-lien—and by extension all Chinese Buddhists—could only feed their forbears indirectly, by means of a Buddhist ritual.

People choosing to feed their forbears through the ritual offering of the yu-lan-p'en—observing a prohibition against animal sacrifice—assumed that, like Mu-lien's mother, their ancestors were *hungry*. To feed hungry beings was a voluntary act; and its charitable character entitled the faithful to religious merit. Previously, in the absence of Buddhist food offerings, blood sacrifices were compulsory; and the adjective *hungry* rarely preceded the term *ghost*. The contrast between involuntary sacrificial rites performed to comply with the rules of a family religion, on the one hand, and voluntary acts performed in the spirit of almsgiving, on the other, helps to explain why people who rejected Buddhism assumed that relic cults went together with observing funerary rites in the company of people who often stood as strangers toward one another.

A vituperative and public complaint against the veneration of Buddhist relics in particular, and against Buddhism in general, by the Tang literary theorist Han Yu (768–824) continued to attract wide public attention long after Han Yu's demise. Indeed, his anti-Buddhist diatribe, written in defense of traditional ancestor veneration, no doubt contributed to the great Chinese persecution of Buddhism in 845. There is evidence to suggest that the document became a minor classic. The enduring public recognition for Han Yu's essay against relic cults in particular and against Buddhism in general may be inferred from the public recognition he received two centuries after his death. For example, consider the actions of Su Chi (1037–1101), a literary figure and member of a group of local elites responsible for establishing lists of licit sacrifices and shrines under the title of *Sacrificial Statutes*. This champion of traditional blood offerings wrote an essay commemorating a shrine built in the Chao Prefecture to honor the figure of Han Yu.[14]

Turn once again to a comparison of China with ancient Palestine. Ancestors could face extermination in both societies. Moses was the only exception; for no one knew where he was interred. Prior to the exile of Jews to Babylonia in 597 BCE, ancestor cults flourished in Judea. At that time the dead enjoyed roughly the same periods of longevity as did their Chinese counterparts. For example, the Book of Exodus (34:7) proclaims that the "iniquity of the fathers" shall be visited "upon the children and the children's children, to the third and fourth generation." It is evil, not the good, that was transmitted from one generation to the next. Moreover, the affliction may have continued for about the same period of time in China, notwithstanding official decrees declaring that seven generations could elapse before the designated time for ritual removal of name-tablets from a Chinese clan hall. But in ancient times most people were illiterate; and ancestral names were easy to forget after about a century. Ordinarily, oral traditions preserve ancestral names for no more than two or three generations.

Prior to the divided monarchy in Palestine (c. 928–722), temples and palaces were in close proximity to one another; and priesthoods and kingships constituted parallel hereditary dynasties. At that time, only lay persons fed the dead. Hereditary priests never made food-offerings to the deceased. Subsequently, in the period of political division, when only Judah, the Southern monarchy, had a temple, priests claimed an exclusive right to perform animal sacrifices to God. Moreover, they repeatedly condemned but could never stop lay people from feeding their ancestors. Meanwhile, in Israel, the northern monarchy, where no temple existed, relic cults flourished in an environment where both rival priesthoods and itinerant holy persons made food offerings to God at altars and shrines called "high places." Israel was especially notable for identifying ritual purity with religious itinerancy, ascetic practices, and voluntary relic cults.

Conversely, temple priests in Jerusalem received prescribed shares of the sacrifices they performed on behalf of the faithful. Like the Brahmins, their counterparts in India, Jewish temple priests were as susceptible to corpse defilement as were the sacrificial structures to which they were bound. Ultimately, Jesus dissociated ritual purity from physical processes when he "cleansed" the Temple. The two founders of the first world religions, Gautama Buddha and Jesus, were itinerant ascetics who, along with their followers, preached for abolition of animal sacrifice. Appropriating the sanctity hitherto ascribed to blood offerings, the two founders, along with their disciples, caused asceticism—understood as a social death, not a physiological demise—to be the chief sign of a holy person. Traveling ascetics, both Buddhist and Christian, ultimately supplanted sacrificial sites and temples, as they crossed cultural lines and ritual boundaries to dispel and even sanctify the sources of defilement at every turn.

Cultural Unity

Throughout the ancient Mediterranean common burial rites—everywhere the mark of a unified culture—ensured the long term persistence of cultural unity in societies where the dead were *not* culturally transformed. At that time, the office of kingship, more than any other institution, assured cultural unity. The contrary was true in imperial China, where kingship served to avert and impede cultural transformation of the dead. As mentioned earlier, according to Professor Mote, the emperor, who "was ritual head of state" stood toward the state as did "the head of every Chinese clan or lineage, by which every person in society was bound to a surname and to family responsibilities." The imperial clan, was

> a model for the maintenance of the *atomized family-based* ancestor veneration that held priority among all the forms of religion in society [italics added].[15]

To my knowledge, kingship never represented a ritually enforced absence of cultural unity in the ancient Mediterranean. More than any other factor, the frequency of pilgrimage in Western Antiquity advanced the ideal of cultural unity. Conversely, the institutional impediments to popular pilgrimage in Imperial China account for an implicit rejection of cultural unity there. Neither cultural unity nor a corresponding cultural identity was ever imposed by royal edicts. As we saw, the Japanese enjoyed a nation-wide circuit of pilgrimage routes by the eleventh and twelfth centuries. Mexico offers perhaps a more dramatic example of a society that made pilgrimage an ultimate instrument for sanctifying the public realm. In this country

> people from every region and from every trade set aside one day each year as *their* day to go on a pilgrimage to the Virgin of Guadalupe, filling most of the days of the year with pilgrimages from some group. For instance there is a Bricklayers' Day, an Electricians' Day, as well as a day for, say, the city of Guadalajara or the state of Chihuahua.[16]

Avoidance of Corpse Defilement: Double Burial and the Rise of World Religions

Double burial, a traditional way to avoid corpse defilement among tribal peoples, reappeared in the form of relic veneration with the rise of Buddhism and Christianity in the so-called axial age—the millennium extending from about 500 BCE to 500 CE. A very brief description of double burial in Borneo prepares the ground for explaining how sanctification of this practice in ancient Palestine and among exiled Jews powerfully contributed to the rise of Christianity. Double burials take many forms. Robert Hertz, an anthropologist famous for his investigation of secondary burial in Borneo, offers a succinct analysis of the practice in a tribal society.

"Corpses are brought back from the graveyard a year or more after death for 'a great feast,' prior to their permanent entombment." According to Hertz, these rites may be interpreted in terms of "the interrelationships between three dramatis personae: the souls of the dead, the living survivors, and the corpse." The dead soul represents "the extinction of the social person," and the survivors "are an expression of the social order."

The soul of the deceased and the body temporarily placed in a graveyard, explains Hertz,

> are related metaphorically.... As the body sinks into corruption, so the soul passes into a wretched state, rejected both by the living and the dead. When only *dry bones* are left, hard and imperishable, the deceased is ready to enter the company of ancestors, and it is this that is celebrated in the "great feast" [italics added].[17]

The redeeming powers ascribed to *dry bones* in Borneo are also present in the biblical description of how secondary burial enhances the life forces inhabiting *dry bones*. The prophet Ezekiel, who was among the Jews exiled to Babylonia in 697 BCE, explains how God guided him in the reform of Jewish burial practices. In a celebrated passage (Ezekiel 37), God speaks through Ezekiel's mouth. The Lord promises to gather all the Jewish bones interred in the Dispersion, and to rebury them in Israel. After Yahweh places the prophet in a valley filled with bones—all of them "very dry" (ritually cleaned of remaining bits of flesh and ready for secondary burial)—the Lord asks the prophet, "Son of man, can these bones live?" (37:13. 3) Addressing the bones, Yahweh promised "to lay sinews on you," to cause "flesh to come upon you, [to] cover you with skin, [to] put breath into you, and you shall live." Ezekiel then heard "a rattling," and the bones came together, "bone to its bone." The prophet "saw them stand up, an exceedingly great host." Hastening to reassure the dead, Yahweh declared "I will open your graves, and raise you from your graves, O my people." About 777 years later Matthew (27:51-52) describes how the bones of the saints came out of their tombs and marched into Jerusalem at the moment of Jesus's resurrection—"and I will bring you home into the land of Israel" (37:1-14). Ancient traditions portray the dead "tunneling through the ground to reach their final resting place." Indeed, Yahweh even lent a hand, and "dug tunnels for them."[18] The disinterment of Jewish bones and their reburial in Jerusalem—a funerary process later described as a resurrection in Matthew—explicitly anticipates the rise of relic cults.

A common dead, common funerary rites, and common reburial in Palestine—often in the hills around Jerusalem—united land, people, and cult. Secondary burial—the disinterment of the bodily remains of Jews buried in the Diaspora and their reburial in the heights around Jerusalem—is a ritual creation of a common dead in a holy land, and it explains why Judaism is the only non-Christian religion in antiquity to have survived to the present day. In fact, the secondary burials in Palestine and their explicit association with a redemptive afterlife prepared the way for Jesus, Judaism's most famous religious reformer. The parallel rise of world empires and world religions, especially Buddhism and Christianity, in the millennium from about 500 BCE to 500 CE are events accompanied by radical changes in mortuary practices associated with the multiplication of relic cults. A widespread devotion for the "dry bones" of saints was especially noticeable by the mid-fourth century. At that time veneration of saints often appeared as a ritual reenactment of secondary burial—practices described as "the digging up, the moving, the dismemberment— quite apart from much avid touching and kissing—of the bones of the sanctified dead."[19] Indeed, not content to bury their dead at the graves of saints, Christians went on to transform martyr tombs for the nonce into altars for celebration of the Mass.

As it impinged on the outside world, "late-antique Christianity *was* shrines and relics"; and this view was shared as far away as Iraq, Iran, and Central Asia by pagans who encountered Nestorian Christians.[20] As Peter Brown shows, the rise to prominence of the Christian Church may be charted by recording pagan reactions to the cult of martyrs. In fact, the progress of martyr cults

> spelled out for pagans a slow and horrid crumbling of ancient barriers [by which people had traditionally tried to mark off the human dead from the living]. In attacking the cult of saints, Julian the Apostate (386–454) mentions the cult as a novelty for which there was no warrant in the gospels; but the full weight of his religious abhorrence comes to bear on the relation between the living and the corpses of the dead that was implied in the

Christian practice: "You keep adding many corpses newly dead to the corpses of long ago. You have filled the whole world with tombs and sepulchers."[21]

If relic translations—a sanctified form of secondary burial—"had not gained a major place in Christian piety," continues Brown, "the spiritual landscape of the Christian Mediterranean might have resembled that of the late Islamic world":

> the holy might have been permanently localized in a few privileged areas, such as the Holy Land, and in "cities of saints," such as Rome. There might have been a Christian Mecca or a Christian Kerbela, but not the decisive spread of major saints, such as Peter and Paul, far beyond the ancient frontiers of the Roman world, as happened in Europe in the dark ages. Elsewhere, the holy might have been tied to the particularity of local graves that enjoyed little or no prestige outside their own region.[22]

In this connection electronically generated maps would be invaluable. A cartography showing the cross-cultural distribution of Christian reliquary shrines and their Buddhist counterparts—stupas, funerary mounds containing relics (called *sarira*) acquired from the cremated remains of the Buddha or a Buddhist saint—located at important pilgrimage shrines throughout Buddhist Asia will provide an historical and geographical guide to the sanctification of secondary burial across a multitude of cultures.

Most of the arguments presented here are founded on the single principle set forth in the first two paragraphs of this essay, namely: collectivities, like individuals, progress from infancy to maturity in differentiated stages. Childhood experiences influence the formation of an adult personality in much the same way that common attitudes toward the dead—seen in funerary rites and mortuary practices—shape the formation of social structures and the development of cultural traits in society. Children live largely in the present. Bed-time stories and fairy tales influence their perceptions of the world in much the same way that myth, not memory, shapes the mentality of tribal societies. As a person matures—in a large-scale society—memory becomes individualized and also intensely social. As one scholar puts it, "I can have very few memories, except perhaps of states of my own inner consciousness, that do not depend in some way upon my membership in a wider community."[23]

Social narratives and collective memories are constructed by the way we describe ourselves to ourselves. A collective identity and a collective memory acquire maturity in the measure people advance from myth to stories about their historical past. A cross-cultural and historical guide to the sanctification of secondary burial would indicate the time required for this or that society to advance from mythological to historical stages of self-description. But with respect to Imperial China, we are faced with a virtual absence of early myths. Ancestor cults either wiped out myth, or ancestor veneration may have historicized myth. In any case, the absence of an early mythical tradition helped to have the dead join with the living in the conduct of daily affairs in ancient and medieval China. As mentioned earlier, people who participate in ancestor cults have always sought a somatic union with the dead. Individuals who feed their ancestors look forward to membership in a community virtually identical to the one they leave at their demise. Figures in stories about neighborhood-oriented netherworlds—even when projected onto the wider-scale visions and stories about events in Chinese hells governed by underworld bureaucracies—differ radically from mythical personages believed to be friends of the gods. Put simply, imaginary figures inhabiting mythical tales are not popular among populations made up by members of private lineages who, intent on feeding their ancestors, sought to avoid the ghosts and demons arising from the corpse defilement incurred by the blood sacrifices they offered at grave sites.

Powerful indirect evidence, originating from a brilliant volume comparing myth and theater in ancient Greece and medieval Japan, supports the view that trans-regional myths simply did not exist in early China. Begin with the term *culture,* understood here to be a collective identity made up of members who contribute to the continued evolution of numerous indigenous realms of meaning. From an external perspective, every realm of meaning is unique. When viewed historically, however, everyone agrees that meanings change over time. The changes themselves and the responses they call forth vary according to the greater or lesser number of people entitled to participate in altering the realms of signification in their society. High percentages of participants strengthen the many factors that cement the bonds uniting individual and collective identity.

Bearing this definition of culture in mind, consider once again the concepts of culture implicit in F.W. Mote's description of the role of an emperor in Imperial China. The Chinese emperor was "a model for the maintenance of an *atomized family-based* ancestor veneration that held priority among *all* forms of religion in society. And unlike his Japanese counterpart, the Chinese emperor did not interact personally with any sector of society" (italics added). By radically diminishing the number of people entitled to participate in expanding and transforming their world of signification, Chinese emperors intensified the gulf separating individual from collective identity. In contrast, considerable evidence from the role of myth, history, and theater in ancient Greece and in medieval Japan shows high percentages of people participating in altering the realms of signification in their respective societies.

According to the *Cambridge History of Japan,* "pilgrimages, work, and the narratives spawned by both, drew people everywhere together into a kind of nationwide network of believers. Having gods in common is a powerful unifying force, and during the middle ages, the Japanese people began for the first time to become shareholders of beloved national gods."[24] From the outset, itinerant holy persons and pilgrims introduced profoundly devotional traits into the history of Japanese relations with their dead. Moreover, a pervasive religious devotion was closely associated with the origins of *noh* theater. And, as we shall see, scholars show striking similarities between Zeami's production of the first *noh* play, *Sanemori,* produced around 1405, and the first Athenian tragedy, Aeschylus's *Persians,* produced in the fifth century BCE, more than two thousand years earlier.

According to Mae J. Smethurst, author of a book entitled *The Artistry of Aeschylus and Zeami: A Comparative Study of Greek Tragedy and Noh,*[25] the religious content of both Greek tragedies and noh and the ambience of religious festivals at which the plays (in case of noh some plays) were performed throughout their histories *distinguish Greek tragedy and noh from much theater of the world* [italics added].[26]

As Smethurst shows, just as there was a close association between the rise of revolutionary Buddhist movements and the founding of Japan's first warrior government, the Kamakura *bakufu* in the 1180s, so the Persian Wars contributed to the rise of a new religious piety among Athenians in the fifth century BCE. A religious militancy in the two societies signifies, among other things, a growing awareness of a common dead, a veneration of common gods, and, especially noteworthy, the appearance of ghosts, representing famous figures from the past, among the *dramatis personae* in both forms of theatrical plays.

At issue here is the relation between early theatrical performances and a convergence of military and religious institutions. Late twelfth-century Japan saw the first warrior government (the *bakufu*), a military regime established in the city of Kamakura. This event marks an early stage in a long-term transition whereby warriors organized as independent bands were transformed into disbanded warriors subject to imperial authority. In the course of these events high army officials offered patronage to new religious groups, such as Zen, to justify an increasingly institutionalized military. A similar phenomenon took place in ancient Athens. Moreover, both warriors and religious figures are prominent among dream figures appearing in the two theatrical productions.

Begin with the literary talents possessed by dream figures in the two types of theatrical productions. Most of the dream figures in *Sanemori* were legendary veterans from famous battles. Events from *The Tale of Heiki,* written in 1371, and famous scenes from the Trojan War in Homer are sources for the most dramatic scenes in the respective plays. A narrative about the cataclysmic Gempi War (1180–1185)—a conflict waged between the Genji and Heiki clans described in *The Tale of Heiki*—provides the specific background for the Japanese play. Moreover, warriors appearing as postmortem dream figures were, in fact, also poets during their life-times. Sanemori, the hero of Zeami's play, "is remembered not only for bravery, but for poetry as well."[27] Also, Aeschylus, a great playwright, per-sonally participated as a member of the heavy infantry (hoplites) in the great naval battles of Artemisium and Salamis in the late summer of 480. A scene in the *Persians* includes a recitation of an eyewitness account of the fateful sea-fights against the Persian vessels—a speech delivered for the ears of an audience (largely made up of men) who had been eyewitnesses to the same events.[28]

Finally, turn now to the theatrical representations of holy personages, accounts of the afterlife, and portrayals of the gods. In both plays military dream figures appear on stage most frequently in the company of a religious personage. In the *Persians* Agememnon and Achilles have roles comparable to those ascribed to the wayfaring holy man Ippen Shonin (1239–1289) and to the figure of Sanemori. The receptivity of the audience to the portrayals of religious figures and heroes on stage testifies, on the one hand, to a close association between religious beliefs and the common experience of warfare. On the other hand, the religious dimensions of warfare help to explain the relatively interchangeable character of terms such as: a *nationalized* dead, a *common* dead, and a *democratized* dead. All three appellations are consistent with a belief in a redemptive immortality. The two playwrights and their audiences manifestly understood from experience that personal subjectivity and religious devotion are eminently communicable states of mind. Noth-ing could be more alien to Chinese traditions.

Dreams and Dream Figures in Cross-Cultural Perspective

The figurative language and feeling-informed images prominent in the-ater and in descriptions of dreams, according to a famous novelist, are made possible by the fact that metaphors

> provide an important hinge between feelings and ideas. Just
> as raindrops need dust motes to condense around, metaphors

need perceptions. Because the mind inhabits the visceral body, and relies on the abstraction of language, it needs a way of embodying thought, of making ideas sensible, of probing the world even when the body is resting.[29]

In ancient India people thought "the universe was like a dream." Myths of illusion "abound in similes and metaphors," explains one scholar, "for they are trying to show how something can be two things at once, and metaphor and simile are language's way of looking at an object in two ways at once or at two objects in one way."[30] The prominence of stories such as *The Monk Who Met the People in His Dream*[31] and the universality of metaphors in Indian discourse and writing went hand in hand with the astonishing frequency of pilgrimage. Unlike Hindus and Japanese, however, the Chinese neither thought dreams to be a source of emotions[32] nor did they consider dreams to be the psychological property of the dreamer. According to the dream records from the Spring and Autumn period (770–481 BCE), "dreams were events that created a bridge between the dreamer and the larger unseen world in which every world was subsumed." Dreams functioned as an awareness of self or an "I" that remains dormant while the body is active. As in the Homeric tales of the free soul, the Chinese dormant self comes to life, as it were, only during dreams, in swoons, or at death. Neither similes nor metaphors are evident in tales about Chinese dreams.

Especially noteworthy is the role of the *hun* and *po* souls in Chinese dream theory. The spiritual soul, called *hun,* which governs the functions of reason, "leaves the body at death and goes to heaven, carrying with it an appearance of the physical form." A dream takes place

> when the connection of the body with the spiritual soul is interrupted. The body lives as long as the material soul dwells in it, but it is doomed to die as soon as it escapes. The spiritual soul may leave the body and enter into communication with spirits; it may freely interview the souls of the departed or have speech with the gods. At the end of the dream the soul returns to the body.[33]

Apart from the Australian aboriginals, the Chinese appear to be the only people who have devised a way to represent dreams pictorially. "From the head of the sleeper radiates a fluttering band or the dream-path in the form of a lane on which are drawn or painted figures appearing in the dreamer's vision." This bit of Chinese iconography is taken from a scene in a Buddhist sutra. It describes a light stream emitted from the Buddha's body, usually from the forehead, that travels upward, lighting up the entire universe, and returns to another part of the Buddha's body. This passage, illustrating the Buddha's omniscience, appears in many opening scenes in Mahayana sutras. Chinese artists paint this scene as a watery stream.[34] This said, the point at issue here is that it would be difficult to imagine a more striking example of the perceived incommunicable nature of Chinese dreams.

The personal dream just described, even if it has religious origins, differs sharply from innumerable dream-messages exchanged between royal officials and city gods at urban incubation temples—a practice attaining a climax toward the end of the fourteenth century. At this time, every town had

> a tutelary god styled 'the father of the walls and moats' and worshiped in a special temple. The city god cares for the welfare of the [city inhabitants], and is the mediator between this and the other life, keeping an account of all the good and evil deeds of his protégés and reporting to these gods of Heaven and Hell. [In the Ming Dynasty (1368–1644)] it was obligatory for all officials of higher ranks ... to pass [their] first nights in the [city god's temple] in order to receive his instructions in a dream. In case of a difficult point of law judges will spend the night in the city god's temple, in the hope that the god will appear to them in a dream and enlighten them on the case in question.... Sometimes a written petition is burned before the altar of the god with proper ritual.[35]

As an instrument of government, temple-sleep was a novel type of ritual to intercede with the gods who mediated between this life and the next. The absence of animal sacrifice, however, requires explanation. Blood offerings made to deceased members of a lineage constitute a practice common to ancestor worship virtually anywhere. But China seems to be the only country where kings, officials, hereditary priests, Taoists, and, by the nineteenth century, even ordinary people required *both* blood offerings *and* procurement of the written word—often obtained by purchase through intermediaries—to communicate with ancestors and the gods. Yet, no animals were sacrificed at incubation rituals. Buddhist influence no doubt accounts for the absence of blood offerings to the dead in temple sleep.

The contrast between incubation practices in Ancient Greece and temple sleep in Ming China illustrates virtually all the major differences distinguishing portable from fixed modes of sanctity. The *Oxford Classical Dictionary* tells us that incubation is "ritual sleep in a sanctuary in order to obtain a dream, mostly for healing." It also explains that:

> Incubation survived the advent of Christianity, and was absorbed into the cult of Byzantine saints as a means of obtaining healing—a phenomenon which survived to modern times.[36]

Thus, unlike the Chinese, ancient Greeks traveled as pilgrims to the temple of Aesclepius and to other healing sanctuaries like Amphiaraion at Oropus and to oracular shrines such as the Aesclepium in the Piraeus. Indeed, the healing inscriptions on the shrine at Epidaurus indicate that devotional piety was associated with healing dreams; and the healing miracles recorded at Christian shrines also testify to a devotional piety. Perhaps one may find parallel phenomena in Buddhism. For example, a visual encounter with the Buddha's Emanation body—the *nirmana kaya*—which places the devotee in the Buddha's immediate presence, may be likened to the god who enters a devotee's dream at an ancient Greek incubation temple. Be that as it may, one thing is certain about Ancient Greek incubation practices. The *Classical Dictionary* tells us that incubation is possible only

> in a culture which believes that at least some dreams can always open communication with the superhuman world; thus, the

experience of incubation [perhaps analogous to an encounter with the *nirmana-kaya*] is always formulated as a real meeting with the god ... [in] a place where the god reveals himself in person to man.

A meeting with an ancient Greek god is an experience that can only be described with the aid of metaphors and similes. And, by extension, so to speak, metaphors used to describe a real experience

tend to liken various experiences which are realistic, if not real, to mythic themes ... which neither the author nor his readers can be assumed to have experienced. This serves not to ground reality in myth; on the contrary, it challenges the primacy of the real.[37]

CHAPTER 4

Germany:
A History of Religious and Cultural Incoherence

A STANDARD HISTORY OF German literature entitled *The Emergence of German as a Literary Language 1700–1755*[1] tells us that modern German literature developed very late. From chapter 9, "The Revival of Metaphor," we learn that metaphor became widespread in literary works only in the second half of the eighteenth century. Resentment created by the belated burgeoning of figurative expression in German literature—and a meteoric rise of theater—helps to explain why, in 1778, Frederick the Great, King of Prussia, complained about the "abominable works of Shakespeare." Expressing outrage at the popularity of the Bard's plays, Frederick grumbled that "the whole audience goes into raptures when it listens to these ridiculous farces worthy of the savages of Canada." More specifically, Frederick objected to

> the porters and gravediggers who come on stage and make speeches worthy of them; after them come the kings and queens. How can such a jumble of lowliness and grandeur, of buffoonery and tragedy, be touching and pleasing?[2]

Frederick's disdain for the popularity of Shakespearean drama reflected the inherent anti-theatrical prejudice built into the contempt that German elites showed toward the development of civil society in western Europe. Frederick's inclination to equate social status with innate virtues testifies to an ideological essentialism that, in some respects, finds a parallel in the writings of the great Prussian philosopher, Immanuel Kant (1724–1804).

Essentialism, the idea that the identity of an object is constituted by what it is, may be exemplified, for example, by Wilhelm Gottfried Leibnitz (1645–1715), who believed that "each object has an individual essence or what is sometimes called a *haecceity*."[3] Frederick's contempt for theatrical performances testifies to a social essentialism.

Meanwhile, moral essentialism, the view that a moral maxim must have an ontological correlate, appears in Kant's extraordinary notions about truth-telling. A debate on this subject began when Benjamin Constant, a French journalist and a well-known public figure, wrote an article asserting that life would be unbearable if everyone told the truth all the time. To support his argument Constant made fun of "a German philosopher" who, in defending the principle of absolute truth-telling, even denied that one had a moral right to deceive a murderer about the hiding place of his intended victim. Constant mistakenly attributed this writing to Kant; in fact the author was a philosopher named Michaelis. Erroneously thinking that Constant's attribution was correct, Kant explained that he could not "remember" where he had printed the piece. To repair this supposed lacuna, Kant, in 1777, published a notorious essay entitled "About the Supposed Right to Lie from Humanitarian Sentiments." In sum, two German scholars, working independently from one another, publicly propounded a preposterous defense of an absolute duty to tell the truth.

The distinguished Kantian specialist, H.J. Paton—known for his work *The Categorical Imperative*[4]— attributed this notorious argument to the philosopher's advanced age and to a desire to defend German philosophy against French ridicule.[5] But neither Kant's alleged senescence—he was seventy-three at the time—nor his patriotism explains why it was Michaelis, not Kant, who first published this absurd argument. Had the writing appeared in France or England, even under the name of a little-known scholar, the article might well have provoked a few published words of learned complaint. Had the same author enjoyed Kant's academic eminence, the essay might have given rise to a public outcry. Yet German scholars remained silent, even though Kant was at the apogee of his fame. The German Academy's absolute silence about absolute truth-telling points to a tacit approval of Kant's views.

Paton also protested that Kant's reasoning was "repugnant to common sense." His remark was prescient, perhaps more so than Paton had suspected. In Germany, "common sense"—translated as *gesunder Menschenverstand* (healthy human understanding)—was a relatively new concept, and several ideological uses of this term were little known in the later eighteenth century. For example, few Germans knew of Thomas Paine's famous pamphlet *Common Sense* (published in January 1776), even though it was "the most incendiary and popular pamphlet of the entire revolutionary era."[6] In England, *common sense* had a considerable variety of usages. Among the meanings listed by the *Oxford English Dictionary* is "the general sense, feeling, or judgment of mankind." In the later eighteenth century western Europeans equated "common sense" with "spontaneous feelings for right conduct" or sentiments produced by a supposed innate capacity for practical judgment. Proponents of this view argued that it was no more possible to "believe" in common sense than it was to "believe" one's own existence.

"Common sense" and *good* sense—terms thought to be the opposite of *non-sense*—referred to aptitudes in two spheres of perceptions and judgments about right and wrong conduct. First, "common sense" was equated with the intuitive judgments guiding practical conduct in everyday affairs. Second, the term also pointed to the faculty of primary truths, a subject central to the debates among common-sense philosophers in France and Scotland. However various their respective points of departure, common-sense philosophers—such as Claude Buffier (1661–1737) in France and Thomas Reid (1710–1796) in Scotland, a contemporary of Kant—all agreed that common sense was a *collective* faculty, usually described as "the general sense, feeling, or judgment of mankind."

In France and Scotland the arguments often turned on how notions of common sense were related to traditional ideas about *belief*. For example, consider the imaginary case of John, a man of ordinary common sense. He is untroubled by a theoretical possibility that the things around him might not continue to exist in his absence. Ordinarily, such a thought would not cross his mind. Suppose John, replying to someone holding a contrary opinion, argues that to give credence to this possibility would be contrary to common sense. Does John's statement testify to a *belief* in the continued existence of the things he observed in a previous moment? In opposing this alleged correlation between common sense and belief, French and Scottish philosophers defined common sense as a state of awareness continuously reified by the spontaneous feelings and innate faculties that guide us in daily life.

Such notions were utterly alien to Kant's essentialist views of morality. This chapter deals with several levels of German essentialism. Some types of essentialism are not intellectual. In Germany belief in demonic spirits represents an essentialism associated with the execution of witches. In contrast to this primitive form of essentialism, Martin Luther manifested a religious essentialism when he proclaimed "the priesthood of all believers." These and several other forms of essentialism were regionally specific, a geographical singularity that afflicted Germany with a profound cultural and political incoherence from the Middle Ages to the Nazi Period. The historical origins of essentialist and non-essentialist readings of "common sense" on the two sides of the Rhine—some exemplified by Immanuel Kant's teachings—help to explain the profound cultural divisions in the Holy Roman Empire.

Backgrounds to Utopia

The most immediate source of controversy about the meaning of "common sense" goes back to the time when Desiderius Erasmus (c.1459–1636), a leading Continental northern Humanist, supervised the printing of *Utopia* (1516), written by Thomas More (1478–1535). Prior to this publication the monastery had always symbolized Europe's notion of an ideal community. *Utopia* offered the first alternative model of an ideal community. Almost everyone in this exemplary society was cremated at death. Only those who led unworthy lives were buried, always in unmarked graves. An absence of identifiable burial sites testified to the irrelevance of a family's social status. People remembered only the *uprightness,* not the names of their forbears. The cremated dead were remarkably mobile, and they were witnesses to the words and actions of the living. Aware that they always lived in the personal presence of their forefathers, the Utopians sedulously avoided secret and dishonorable deeds.

Miracles were not only frequent in Utopia, they also occurred "without the assistance of nature." Sometimes, "in great and critical affairs [the Utopians] pray publicly for a miracle, which they very confidently look for and obtain."[7] They prayed to God for a miracle rather than assisting Him in its performance by visiting a holy shrine. The statement about miracles occurring "without the assistance of nature" indicates that, in Thomas More's day, few things in "nature" contributed more than pilgrimage to the performance of miracles. The Utopians lived in the presence of their dead, not in the memory of departed souls. People experienced time as hope; duration did not exist among those living in a perpetual present. But outside Utopia, in historical societies, where the dead are remembered, the deeds of earlier generations often influence private and public behavior in the present. Previous actions recounted in books and frequently depicted in paintings caused men to follow the passage of their society from one period to the next.

According to Thomas More and Erasmus, nothing is more conducive to war than the memory of real or imagined wrongs committed by one country against another. The two scholars adamantly opposed a prevailing idea that the word *peace* should refer to an absence of conflict within the borders of only one country. To nationalize the concept of peace, to give kings an exclusive right to wage war abroad, according to More and Erasmus, was to deny that peace was a principle generic to the government of man. The equity and civility binding a people to its prince ought also to control the behavior of sovereign states toward one another.

Some humanists defended Erasmus's universal principles of international concord, while others argued in favor of the predominantly French *étatist* version of the same subject. Meanwhile, a multitude of German Prince Bishops and military officials in the Holy Roman Empire ignored such issues. Rejecting all humanist views, the clerical and military leaders of the Empire sought to assimilate the Imperial Knights and the Imperial Church so as to allow princes and prelates to represent a single political authority. To maintain that warriors and ecclesiastical officials should hold interchangeable offices was to place penance at the center of public affairs, and to repudiate the principles of equity essential to humanist concepts of peace—not to mention the rejection of an established western European *étatist* doctrine separating Church and State. In the Holy Roman Empire the term "defense of the peace," when taken in its broadest sense, referred chiefly to the continued integrity of prevailing legal relations.

Even in Kant's youth, German intellectuals continued to think that the word "society" meant little more than the sum of legal relations—a precise analogue to the predominantly juristic notions of religion prevailing in the Holy Roman Empire since the revolutionary rise of Protestantism. After the Religious Peace of Augsburg (1555) and after the abdication of Charles V—leaving the imperial office and the Hapsburg lands to his brother Ferdinand I, in 1556—religion in Catholic Germany appeared, as one scholar puts it, to be "a legal institution subject to administrative control and changes in territorial location."[8]

W.C. Oxtoby points out that, contrary to western Europeans, Germans do not distinguish between the adjectives *holy* and *sacred*.[9] Only a few among the many linguistic facts offered by Oxtoby are relevant here. First,

> *Sacred,* a past participle of a now-archaic verb *sacren,* meaning "to consecrate," implicitly commits the speaker or writer merely to a description of human veneration, whereas *holy* may more likely imply that the user of the term holds that the object in question has indeed been hallowed by God…. [Here] *holy* is much more exclusively a participant's term. Thus we say "the Holy Bible" in a context where the book is treated with reverence, but in referring to others' scripture we are comfortable with expressions such as "the sacred books of the East."

Second, German is a language "in which *the holy* and *the sacred* are one and the same." Technically, the word *heilig* can cover both the participant's semantic field of the English *holy* as well as the observer's connotation of the English *sacred.* The inter-changeable nature of the two terms offers unlimited opportunities for distortion. For example, explains

Oxtoby, "the domain of authority claimed in Latin by the *sacrum impe-rium Romanum* became semantically extended when rendered through German as the Holy Roman Empire, a construal that exalted German imperial pretensions." But this particular example may be pressed too far, explains Oxtoby; "for, after all, a divine sanction for the power of the state *was* claimed."[10] Oxtoby's words of caution, however, apply only to Catholics, not, for example, to Martin Luther's protest that to call an empire holy made as much sense as to claim that a pious cobbler produces Christian shoes. Some languages have no equivalent for either *holy* or *sacred.* Faced with the absence of any correlative terms in the target language, the Bible translator "might render *Holy Spirit* with an expression like *clean ancestors.*" Concepts of purity and lineage, often associated with the term *heilig,* will play an important role in the history of German religious and cultural development.

Moreover, the multivalent meanings ascribed to *heilig* may have complicated Luther's early efforts—beginning with his ninety-five theses against indulgences—to dissociate spiritual life from manifestly secular concerns. Reputedly, Luther tacked up a copy of his ninety-five statements against indulgences on October 31, 1517. In 1520 a papal Bull, *Exsurge Domine,* condemned Luther for heresy. In early December of the same year Luther

> burned that bull at the gates of Wittenberg, along with the works of Johann Eck [of the Bavarian University of Ingolstadt] and volumes of canon law that were the foundation of papal administration in the Church.[11]

Amid the enormous public agitation that followed, Luther published his *Address to the Christian Nobility of the German Nation* in German, not Latin; and the writing was delivered "to those in charge of decision making in the Empire." This was the most popular of Luther's early public addresses. Declaring that the pope, "far from being God's representative on earth, was an imposter put in place by the Devil, the Antichrist," Luther set in motion uncontrollable forces. This address is often called a nationalist book. But one has to be careful to avoid misunderstanding the feeling to which Luther was appealing in his book: the "nation" in his title was the sacred medieval institution of the Holy Roman Empire and its privileged nobility, not the totality of German speakers in Europe, and he was calling for one universal set of representatives of God, the emperor and his nobility, to punish the crimes of another universal claimant to universal representation, the pope.[12]

Developing theological doctrine while embroiled in continuous public controversy, Luther ultimately divorced religion, which he defined as *faith,* from society. According to Luther, the "clergy who administered Communion were not set aside to be special priestly beings; that idea was part of the Roman cheat. Every faithful Christian was a priest."[13] French and English Protestants, many of whom ultimately emigrated to North America, all believed in a bodily resurrection. In contrast, Luther said little about this issue. Insisting on the priesthood of all believers and denying the sacrificial functions of the Mass, Luther identified redemption with Divine Love. Christ's promise, as set forth in "the plain words of Scripture," to forgive the sins of the faithful had, in Luther's view, made resurrection a moot and difficult issue.[14] Luther's silence about a bodily resurrection and the Reformer's insistence on the priesthood of all believers set faith in opposition to ecclesiastical institutions; and thereby effectively divorced religion from society.

Meanwhile, Catholic notions of Empire caused clerical and imperial offices to become parts of a single overarching religious-political authority. In both instances an indifference to matters of social import helped to persuade Germans for centuries that values existed in a realm external to society. The tendency to dissociate value judgments from both individual activities and also from wider social processes obscured the distinction between intrinsic and instrumental values, and thereby divorced individuals from the collective experience people develop in social intercourse. Immanuel Kant's ethical theories, perhaps more clearly than any other work, exemplify the German doctrinal refusal to allow social experience to assist individuals to make an easy transition from ideal to overt behavior.

The Kantian actor recognizes no moral law outside his own judgment. In every moral decision he must act as if he were a cosmic legislator about to promulgate a universal law. Conceiving moral life to originate in sources outside the sphere of social or cultural fact, Kant describes an autonomous moral will—it determines itself entirely within itself—that imposes on the individual an absolute duty to transcend his own social environment in the pursuit of the goals of universality, completeness, and totality. In this context, return for a moment to Frederick the Great's specific complaints in his discussion about the "abominable works of Shakespeare." The Monarch objected to

> the porters and gravediggers who come on stage and make speeches worthy of them; after them come the kings and queens. How can such a jumble of lowliness and grandeur, of buffoonery and tragedy be touching and pleasing?

The Prussian king's concern to maintain a cultural environment compatible with the hierarchical structure of society—such as existed prior to the explosion of literary works in the later eighteenth century—reflects a mind-set analogous to the profoundly asocial implications of Kant's notorious nonsense about "The Supposed Right to Lie from Benevolent Motives." The implications following from such fierce hostility to the institutions of civil society—manifested above all in Frederick's militant anti-theatrical prejudice—are suggested by the contrast between conflicting interpretations of the word *freedom* on the two sides of the Rhine during the 1950s. In the West "freedom" meant the right to act according to one's own desires and moral convictions. In contrast, George Iggers, citing numerous authorities, explains that Germans interpreted *freedom* "in terms of individual spiritual growth rather than in terms of political participation."[15]

It seems clear that Frederick II's contempt for Shakespearean drama and Kant's defense of absolute truth-telling—reflecting, on the one hand, an essentialist concept of social status and, on the other, an essentialist concept of morality—are closely related to the subsequent conflation of political freedom with individual spiritual development in early twentieth-century

Germany. In the eighteenth century, Kantian philosophy and Prussian militarism showed no trace of the socially bonding traits immanent in western European views of "common sense." In sum, two major forces contributed to the development of movements seeking to substitute personal piety for participation in public affairs. First, however preposterous in its initial formulation, Kant's argument for absolute truth-telling is, in a modified form, an ideal that was entirely in keeping with the spirituality expressed in the Lutheran belief in a "priesthood of all believers." Second, the view that a spirit of "humanity" may be achieved by a sustained search for truth also reflects an attitude influenced by Lutheran piety. And a civic formulation of this view in the late eighteenth century—to be cited shortly—appealed to large sectors of eighteenth-century educated German Protestants.

Conversely, such views were utterly alien to common-sense philosophers on the other side of the Rhine. The moral qualities people ascribed to spontaneous feelings for right conduct and possession of common sense were thought to be as natural as the possession of hands and feet. People who advanced the cause of a universal common sense argued that belief in absolute virtues and absolute forms of turpitude were necessarily private convictions, and therefore contrary to public policies contributing to the advancement of civil society. Among its many other meanings, the word *common* also signifies: "of or belonging to the community at large or to a community or corporate public" *(OED)*. In this sense, to cite Oscar Wilde, *common* feelings of patriotism may be seen as "the substitution of a universal for an individual feeling." And in this context, explains Wilde, "it is also worth noticing that Shakespeare's first and last successes were both historical plays."[16]

Conflicting Notions of Humanity on the Two Sides of the Rhine

Defenders of common sense generally followed some, but by no means all, the principles that Bernard Mandeville proposed in his most famous work, *The Fables of the Bees: Or, Private Vices, Public Benefits* (1714), based on a satirical poem entitled "The Grumbling Hive: or Knaves turned Honest." According to Mandeville, people should be accepted as they are. Everyone must recognize that private vices—such as pride, envy, and avarice—often advance industry, expand trade, promote prosperity, and generally contribute to the public welfare. Adopting a few of Mandeville's multiple proto-utilitarian arguments, the defenders of "common sense" thought that many of the "moral inconveniences" Mandeville described would gradually disappear. Mere common sense, they argued, suggests that increasing levels of prosperity will promote feelings of humanity, raise the level of humanitarian activities, and thereby advance sentiments of civility and friendship. According to the French *Encyclopédie, humanité* "is a sentiment of good will." It inspires us to be "tormented by the sufferings of others and by the need to assuage them." *Humanité* makes us "better friends, better citizens, better spouses."

Passages declaring that humanitarian feelings contribute to public benevolence and domestic concord—largely contemporary with the writings of Kant and Frederick II—conflicted dramatically with German concepts of *Humanität,* defined as a search for truth. A famous lecture by Werner Richter describes the late eighteenth-century notion of *Humanität* as a belief,

> that out of a search for truth ... from a belief in truth, human individuality receives its formation automatically and that formation will necessarily bring forth the self-realization of all inherent and noble dispositions. The totality of human powers should be reflected in the single individual, a totality elevating the human type as well as contributing to the harmonious cultivation of the single personality.[17]

The conviction that *Humanität* is achieved from a sustained search for truth—a view influenced by centuries of Lutheran piety—was entirely compatible with the spirit, if not with an unqualified acceptance of Kant's philosophical convictions about absolute truth-telling. The following section discusses massacres of Jews and a wider militant anti-Semitic ideology in the Catholic regions of Bavaria and South Germany; pogroms prevailed in these lands throughout the medieval and early modern periods. A final section describes how the anti-Semitic character of Bavarian and South German pilgrimage practices—nourished by traditions of fixed sanctity and a deep fear of witches, ghosts, and other demonic spirits—merged with North German tendencies to confuse personal piety with political freedom. The disastrous conditions following military defeat in World War I made possible a confluence of Prussian militarism—and a traditional ideology dissociating value judgments from the collective experience of the wider society—with Bavarian and South German anti-Semitic agitations. In sum, the following pages discuss the medieval movements contributing to the persistence of radical religious and cultural divisions throughout late medieval and much of modern German history.

In a study entitled *Apocalypticism in the Wake of the German Reformation*,[18] Robin Barnes shows that a magical, apocalyptic expectancy—built into the Lutheran belief in God's transcendence and in the utter contingency of human life—united faith and cosmology in the non-Romanized regions of Germany until the age of Rene Descartes (1596–1650). Just as belief in a sudden dissolution of the present dominated religious life in North and Central Germany, so in Catholic Germany, especially in Bavaria, a multitude of miracle books and legends testifies to a reflorescence of late medieval pilgrimage during the seventeenth and eighteenth centuries. No apocalyptic message is contained in these tales; nor is the Armageddon suggested in other supernatural events recounted in German Counter-Reformation propaganda.[19] Yet both Catholics and Protestants, each in their own way, kept witches and other evil spirits at bay throughout the early modern period. Witchcraft practices continued in West Germany, especially in Bavaria, at least into the 1960s. As one scholar puts it,

> Only West Germany seems to need an Archive for the "Investigation of Contemporary Witchcraft Superstition," founded in Hamburg in 1920 and still active. In the late 1960s, several dozen crimes related in some way to witchcraft were still reported annually in West Germany.[20]

A continued presence of evil spirits—personified by witches, Jews, gypsies, and other apotropaic figures in post-war Germany—is not usually associated with the apocalyptic expectations of a previous age. Yet a recent book—*Destroying the World to Save It: Aum Shinrikyo, Apocalyptic Violence, and the New Global Terrorism*[21]—by Robert Jay Lifton shows that apocalyptic movements seeking to exterminate "unclean" people are still alive and well in contemporary Japan. Fear of contaminated beings is one of the oldest human emotions, and it continues to haunt us today.

The Structure of Medieval German Piety: A Historical Synopsis

In three studies, published in 1979, 1980, and 1988, I discussed the distribution of more than one thousand pilgrimage sites established before the Reformation in a land area corresponding roughly to the territories governed by Germany in 1939, excluding Austria and Czechoslovakia.[22] This section, especially the statistical presentation, relies heavily on these publications; but the general theory set forth in the initial chapter of this volume is only partially related to the material discussed here. Begin with a fundamental question: Why did Germans find no martyrs among the 100,000 people killed in the Great Peasants' War (1524–1525)? Even Catholic populations in the Empire perceived no martyrs among themselves; yet many Catholics died for their faith during the Reformation. Martyrdom had little ideological resonance in the Holy Roman Empire, largely because early medieval Germans imported most of their saints from abroad. Some medieval clerics argued that the discovery of even one German saint would be celebrated as a miraculous event.[23] To be sure, this statement ignores figures such as the canonized archbishops of Cologne; and Hildegard of Bingen (1098–1179), "the sibyl of the Rhine," venerated as a living saint. But Cologne and Bingen, located in the extreme western part of Germany, were situated in a region deeply influenced by the piety prevailing on the other side of the Rhine. In fact, Germans venerated a multitude of non-German saints; and most of them were martyrs. The two phenomena are really different aspects of the same problem. Since martyrs were plentiful among the foreign saints who were venerated in Germany, a dearth of German martyrs—not being ascribable to a difference in the concept of sanctity—can only be attributed to a paucity of native German saints.

Prior to the 1090s relics existed at the vast majority of European saint shrines. At that time, however, the non-Romanized regions of Germany had few shrines dedicated to saints. The reason is clear: relic veneration never found firm footing in lands where the indigenous populations had been converted to Christianity by force of arms. For example, Charlemagne (768–814) showed unusual levels of ruthlessness in his numerous wars to convert the Saxons, most of them unsuccessful. On one occasion, the Emperor revenged a massacre of young noble Franks by decapitating a reported four thousand Saxon prisoners in a single day.[24] Later, in the 1200s, the Teutonic Order of the Knights intensified the eastward expansion of Christianity. In their campaigns to convert pagan peoples by the sword—called *Heidenmissionen* ("missions to convert the pagans")—these warrior monks showed a level of ferocity comparable to the savagery later shown by the Mongol hordes. Invasions launched in the name of Christ against populations in the lands colonized in the North and in territories east of the Elbe continued down to the eve of the Reformation, and persisted even later in Prussia, Courland, Livonia, and Estonia. Unable to perceive saints either among their conquerors or among their own people, subjugated populations founded few pilgrimage sites to this type of celestial patron. For example, a German missionary bishop who told the pagan peoples of Wagria "as you alone differ from the religion of all, so are you subject to the plunder of all"[25] gave his audience every reason to shun pilgrimage sites dedicated to saints.

After 1200, however, people in the colonized lands of northern and eastern Germany built shrines to Christ and Mary. The number of sites increased in the fourteenth century, and finally attained an apogee in the fifteenth century. Since neither Christ nor Mary were thought to have left corporeal remains, it is no surprise to discover a specialist in Pomeranian Church history declare that "it is unmistakable ... relic worship in

Pomerania was never so popular *(volkstumlich)* as, for example, in southern territories."[26] Moreover, the Cistercians and Premonstratensians—monastic orders responsible for establishing Christian practices in the colonized regions—prohibited the use of relics as cult objects in churches, at least in the earlier history of their Orders.[27] According to R.W. Southern, isolated Cistercian monasteries, far removed from the towns, cities, and castles, were especially notable for

> the severity of their internal discipline, the discouragement of learning, the plainness of ritual, [and] the *absence of relics* [italics added].[28]

Missions to convert the pagans were especially numerous during the maelstrom of the Interregnum (1254–1273). Looking at Rome from the Empire in the light of two centuries of dealing with pontiffs who fulminated bulls and hurled anathemas against Holy Roman Emperors, Germans saw the issuance of indulgences to the so-called crusaders who were waging a perpetual war against them to be a license to wreak havoc in the name of Christ and to bless the martyrs who died in an iniquitous cause. The Interregnum also denied central direction to the military campaigns to convert the heathen; and the local authorities in charge of colonization during the Empire's eastward expansion found it difficult to declare a holy war against the non-Christian peoples residing in their own jurisdictions. These officials acted as invaders and local tyrants; and they could not promote an acceptance of indulgences among the peoples of non Romanized Germany. Widespread hatred of indulgences as symbols of tyranny and contempt for the supposed martyrdom of alleged saints at pilgrimage shrines ultimately contributed to the immense popular support that Luther received when he condemned the papal issuance of indulgences a little more than two centuries later. In Germany it is difficult to find any martyrs. Not even the Teutonic Knights, who were warrior monks, perceived a single martyr among their fallen brethren during more than three centuries of crusade. This fact, when taken together with the Lutheran propensity to make private experience the foundation for theology, partially explains why the martyr ideal never influenced German patriotic sentiment in the modern age. No tomb to an unknown soldier—a figure who now personifies a national martyr—appeared in Germany, not even after the enormous casualties suffered in the great war of 1914–1918.

To confirm these general observations I established a sample list of 1,036 German pilgrimage shrines dedicated to Christ, Mary, and Saints prior to the Reformation. They show widely divergent ratios from one region to another; and our purpose is to discover the implications that flow from their geographical distribution. Consider first the lands extending north from a line running roughly from Aachen to Dusseldorf to Frankfurt on the Oder—the so-called Benrather Line separating Low German in the north from Middle and High German in the south. Beginning with the Bishopric of Munster and the province of Westphalia, fourteen of a total of sixty-six sites were dedicated to saints. In Pomerania only one out of fifteen, and not a single one of the twenty-one shrines in Branden-burg, none of the seven in Mecklenburg, nor any of the eight in Prussia, and merely one of the six pilgrimage places in Lower Saxony had patron saints. Finally, of the nineteen sites in Lower Saxony, from the same number in Schleswig and of the seventeen in Silesia (going somewhat below the line east of the Elbe), there were four patron saints in the first, four in the second, and two in the third region. In sum, a saint appears at merely twenty-six of the 178 pilgrimage places in north and eastern Germany, fourteen of them concentrated in the subsequently Catholic Munster-Westphalia—a ratio of almost one to seven. Outside Munster-Westphalia the ratio is close to one to fifteen.

In contrast, Bavaria in the south—meaning here Upper and Lower Bavaria, the Innviertel and the Upper Palatinate—boasted 151 saints out of a total of 313 sites. In Franconia 60 out of 148, and in Swabia and Baden together 101 out of 236 shrines were dedicated to saints. In sum, saints worked their wonders at 312 or almost 45 percent of a total of 697 shrines. The ratio in Hesse, the Middle Rhine, and Thuringia was about the same; moreover, nearly one shrine in three was dedicated to a saint in the Rhine Palatinate. Also, the southern lands that remained Catholic during the Reformation not only show many saint shrines, but all regions with an abundance of saint shrines also have numerous pilgrimage places dedicated to other celestial patrons. Thus in the north, Catholic Munster-Westphalia produces a configuration that is virtually identical to the distribution of shrines in the jurisdiction of its confessional counterparts to the south. Conversely, no shrines to saints appear among the relatively few pilgrimage sites in regions that later turned Protestant during the Reformation. Never do we find a random distribution: either there were many or there were few shrines to saints; and this typological asymmetry varied either directly or inversely with the arithmetic distribution of pilgrimage places dedicated to Mary and Christ.

New Facts and Further Reflections

Learned commentaries about the distribution and character of German pilgrimage sites prior to the Reformation have considerably widened the nature and the scope of inquiry since my own publications on this subject. The sheer labor of locating more than a thousand pilgrimage sites—listed in the appendices of a work I published in 1980—hid several devotional issues associated with specific sub-groups of shrines. At that time the general picture was at once novel and massively evident. Several differences in the forms of local piety, especially those revealed by art historians, escaped learned attention. No doubt this is why George Hunston Williams, Hollis Professor of Divinity at Harvard, devoted only a single paragraph to cartography in his ample commentary on other aspects of my publication. As Williams put it:

> A striking support for Rothkrug's principal thesis about why two thirds of Germany went Lutheran is gained from leafing through the scholarly, also pious manual of German saints by Jakob Torcy, *Lexikon der deutschen Heiligen* (Cologne, 1959) with its extensive literature cited and with one map to aid the user to locate the places of birth and veneration of the saints popular in Germany. The single map covers the whole of modern France, Belgium, the Netherlands, and Switzerland but includes, even of the Federal Republic, only the Rhineland and

western Bavaria! Rothkrug is visually vindicated by a canon scholar of Cologne![29]

Showing that a rarity of saint shrines helps to explain why "two thirds of Germany went Lutheran" is one thing. It is quite another, however, to account for both the similarities and the differences between "Bleeding Hosts and their Contact Relics in Late Medieval Northern Germany"[30] as opposed to the piety represented by the numerous, often highly differentiated bleeding-host pilgrimage sites in Bavarian south Germany. The central theme of my more recent publications is that population growth and shifting patterns of peregrination reveal profound changes in popular notions of sanctity. Mitchell Merback has recently confirmed with great detail this thesis in a chapter contributed to a book, noteworthy for the contributions of numerous scholars addressing the experience and the iconography of late medieval pilgrimage in Northern Europe and the British Isles.[31]

Crusades and Equine Communions in the Rural South

A relatively small number of Germans participated in European crusades to the Holy Land. Most of them were ministerials; and these warriors were concentrated in Romanized Germany, principally in the Maine-Rhine and Danube valleys, in Thuringia, in Franconia, and in the lands to the south. In these regions Imperial government was organized around vast numbers of castles built in the civil wars that began during the great Investiture struggle—a long series of disputes between popes and emperors that continued from Henry IV's rejection of papal authority in 1076 to the Concordat of Worms in 1122.[32] Ministerials served in military and administrative posts for the Emperor, for bishops, for abbots or free nobles, even for towns. Neither villains nor free vassals, neither serfs nor free knights, often powerful lords of unfree status, ministerials formed a class of warriors and civil servants who, by the twelfth and thirteenth centuries, had become so large that "they vastly outnumbered the old nobility."[33]

Between 1096 and 1146 ministerials made up 29 percent of the German contingents to the Holy Land, from 1149 to 1191 they constituted 75.5 percent, and finally, they made up 97 percent of the German crusaders from 1192 to 1250. These warriors were the German counterparts of the French *juvenes*—the disinherited younger sons of French nobility. They too formed "the cutting edge of feudal aggressiveness." They "fanned the fires of trouble in areas of instability and provided the best contingents for distant expeditions."[34] To assert their claims to social superiority these sons and grandsons of serfs became literary devotees. Like their French counterparts, ministerials pursued poetry in quest of a fortunate marriage, transforming the south into Germany's sole center for love poetry, the *Minnesang*, between 1170 and 1250.[35] The ministerial mind-set is perhaps best described by an illuminating passage from a contemporary French troubadour:

> Behold! without renouncing our rich garments, our station in Life, courtesy, and all that pleases and charms we can obtain Honor down here and joy in Paradise. To conquer glory by fine deeds and escape hell; what count or king could ask more? No more is there need to be tonsured or shaved and lead a hard life in the most strict order if we can revenge the shame which the Turks have done us. Is this not truly to conquer at once land and sky, reputation in the world and with God?[36]

Forming the virtual totality of German Crusaders, most of these producers and consumers of love poetry were emancipated from their servile status in the half century following the Interregnum (1254–1273). The Emperor's ministerials, located chiefly in Swabia, Franconia, and in the western Rhine and Middle Rhine valleys, became *de facto* rulers of petty holdings and bailiwicks which they had carved out of the political ruins of the post-Hohenstaufen Empire. But in lands lying east of the river Lech, Bavarian ministerials served a powerful duke who only granted them hereditary rights to noble status. Subsequently, the descendants of hereditary ministerials—composing almost the entire Bavarian nobility after about 1350[37]—continued to aspire to the quasi-independent status enjoyed by their Franconian and Swabian brethren. Ultimately, they rose to fight for political independence in the famous *Lowlerkrieg,* when they were crushed by Duke Albrecht IV in 1488.

Meanwhile, return for a moment to about 1300. At that time, Bavarian ministerials sought to consolidate and to solemnize their newly acquired hereditary aristocratic status. Toward this end they assimilated old imperial rituals with the ideology of Crusades, and injected these innovations into common pilgrimage practices. The organization of local crusades launched against Jews may have been the most spectacular product of this revived spirit of religiously inspired conquest. To enlist the peasantry in these enterprises, ministerials introduced a species of equine communions. The new ritual importance ascribed to the horse emphasized the supposed missionary spirit that informed the ministerial war against Jews. On the feasts of Saint Leonard and Saint George, who were the celestial patrons of crusading knights in previous centuries, peasants brought smartly decorated horses to churches specially equipped to offer them communion. At first a priest blessed the animals with holy water. After this introductory ritual, the peasants led their horses into the church through special doors built for this purpose. Often they rode their steeds down through the center of the church. And, after much effort, they finally compelled their animals to look directly at either the exposed Host or at the "windows" of the monstrance housing it.[38] The ceremony was a variant of a practice called the *Umritt.* The earliest *Umritte* go back to Ottonian times when Saxon Kings, on accession to the throne, embarked on ritualized *Umritte* of the Empire, receiving everywhere pledges of obedience from their subjects.[39]

Equine communes and horse pilgrimages multiplied prodigiously after 1300. One scholar counts more than two hundred sites established for *Umritte* in Bavaria,[40] many of them constituting a distinctive form of pilgrimage.[41] In the fifteenth century the Upper Bavarian village of Dietramzell was

> distinguished for its horse Umritte. Peasants arrived from as far
> as four hours' ride with specially decorated wagons on the Sun-
> day following the feast of Mary Magdalene. Upon arrival they
> immediately broke into a sharp trot, driving three times around

the Saint Leonhard's pilgrimage church amid the chanted prayers of those sitting in the wagons.[42]

A recent historical *Volkskunde* map describes Bavaria as an *"Überaus umrittfreudiges Land"* (a land delighting exceedingly in *Umritt*). The map lists as the chief forms of the ritual: the *Osterritt, Georgritt, Pfingstritt, Fronleichnamsritt, Leonhardiritt, Martiniritt, Stephanritt, Johannritt, Blasiusritt*.[43] Unlike occasional *Umritte* organized in Westphalia or elsewhere in the Empire, the Bavarian and South German ceremony developed as an integral part of popular, largely peasant peregrination.

Rural Pogroms in Defense of the Eucharist and Mary, Lady Victor of All God's Urban Battles

The immense role of peasants in performing equine communions indicates a predominantly rural ceremony; and pilgrimage shrines associated with these rituals were dedicated to the Bleeding Host. For example, consider the history of pilgrimage to the Benedictine monastery of Scheyern, some thirty miles north of Munich. About 1155 Count Konrad I of Dachau donated a particle of the True Cross to the monastery; and the monks established a shrine to this relic from the Crucifixion. All authorities agree that medieval processions to the monastery's holy particle were the source of Scheyern's later pilgrimage renown—reaching its height when "more than 200 horsemen" rode their mounts around the county, circling the entire pilgrimage area, "from before five A.M. to five in the evening."[44] At Scheyern the *Umritt* was a later phenomenon, appearing for the first time only in the fourteenth or fifteenth century. Nevertheless, the *Umritt* restored to the holy particle, in a new aristocratic form, the crusading significance it originally enjoyed in 1155. Scheyern's ultimate achievement in equine ritual grandeur in the Counter-Reformation was modest when compared to the 7,055 horsemen who in 1756 participated in the famous Holy Blood *Umritt,* known as the *Blutritt,* celebrated since 1490 on "Bloody Friday" at the miracle of the Bleeding Host housed in the Benedictine monastery of Weingarten.[45]

Urban centers show a precisely parallel process in the history of Virgin worship. The story begins with two series of events: first, the large-scale massacres of Jews by mobs under the leadership of an obscure Franconian noble, called Rindfleisch, in 1298; second, the numerous fanatical bands, known as *Armleders,* who exterminated human life in literally hundreds of south German Jewish communities from 1336 to 1339.[46] To celebrate their triumphs over the descendants of Israel these armies of *Judenschläger* (Jew killers) erected monuments on Ghetto ruins in, for example, Nurnberg, Eger, Wurzberg, Bamberg, Regensburg, Rothenburg, Munich, Heidelberg, Ingolstadt, Cologne, and Amberg.[47] All these monuments were erected to the "Queen of Heaven," later known as *Siegerin aller Gottes Schlachten* (Lady Victor of all God's Battles). To summarize the several implications following from these events, it is helpful to cite a passage by the art historian Mitchell B. Merback:

> By the mid-fourteenth century a pattern emerged: fanatical mobs like those led by the Franconian nobleman Rindfleisch or the so-called *Armleders* (named for the leather patches worn on their sleeves) marched into Jewish communities, exterminated the inhabitants and established shrines on the sites of razed synagogues. Where urban populations performed pogroms against their Jews, the resulting shrines were dedicated to Mary, now worshipped as the "conquering Virgin" *(Siegerin aller Gottes Schlachten,* or Lady Victor of All God's Battles).

·◆·

In the countryside, by contrast, sites of massacres were transformed into shrines to the suffering Christ: Country folk slaughtered Jews for Christ; urban populations massacred them for Mary.

·◆·

The calamitous fall of Constantinople to the Turks in 1453 brought the heathen to the gates of Europe and resulted in an unprecedented public agitation for crusades. The wish to repel the Turk intensified crusading zeal throughout south Germany, and led people to promote unusual forms of peregrination to enlist celestial forces in their holy war. Again, Rothkrug's survey of shrines shows Austria, Bohemia, but especially Bavaria to be the "chief centre where churches and shrines dedicated to the Virgin continued for centuries to symbolize the spirit of pogrom and crusade." In these regions pilgrimage processions continued to include the slaughter of Jews into the sixteenth century.[48]

In a recent book entitled *Art and Architecture of Late Medieval Pilgrimage in Northern Europe and the British Isles,*[49] Merback and many other scholars contributed chapters on the religious, cultural, and artistic influences of late medieval pilgrimage. At the beginning of a chapter entitled "Channels of Grace: Pilgrimage Architecture, Eucharistic Imagery, and Visions of Purgatory at the Host-Miracle Churches of Late Medieval Germany,"[50] Merback points out that:

> Of the religious practices that could become lodestones of collective identity—and collective perceptions—in the two-and-a-half centuries before the Reformation, pilgrimage was arguably the most important.[51]

To assess the role of images at a particular shrine, argues Merback, the art historian must distinguish between elite and popular forms of peregrination. Among the former were "journeys ... to shrines of high prestige, at high cost, across long distances ... to Jerusalem, Rome, and Santiago de Compostella, and supra-regionally to ... well-known destinations [such as] Einseideln, Wilsnack, Aachen, and Canterbury." In this type of pilgrimage private experience "takes center stage." In rural communities, however, pilgrimage was very often a *corporate* undertaking; and the efficacy of the rites it encompassed "was, in a sense, vouchsafed by a thoroughgoing and often obligatory communal participation." In the German empire, where political authority was most fragmented, pilgrimage shrines were "regional identification points." The shrine and community constituted a single sociological unit.[52] Within this specific framework of popular perceptions of religious images, Merback describes how the multi-faceted nature of host relics and their relationships to communal pilgrimages, especially in the Churches that housed them, centered on creating "a channel of grace." The blessings ascribed to a particular relic's power had both a downward and an upward direction. In some instances pilgrims visualized dead souls *(armeseelen)* imprisoned either "beneath the paving stones" or in some appalling "sepulchral space." Conversely, other relics allowed pilgrims to imagine liberated souls moving toward heaven. The negative and positive aspects of these practices were regionally distinct; and their geography is entirely consistent with the Bleeding Host shrines and crusading horse pilgrimages described in this chapter.

An Upward Displacement of Sanctity

Return for a moment to the fact that the German word *heilig* can cover both the participant's semantic field of the English *holy* as well as the observer's connotation of the English *sacred.* An inability to distinguish participatory from observational perceptions of religious ritual originates in the *impersonal* nature of the religious practice itself. At issue here are the personality attributes ascribed to the concept of sanctity. Sacrifices offered to ancestors in medieval China had a commemorative function, identifying the practitioner as a member of a recognized lineage. In this instance, a person affirms his identity by commemorating a deceased family member. No commemorative features are associated with killing Jews and establishing pilgrimage shrines dedicated either to the bleeding body of Jesus or to a warrior image of the Virgin Mary. Chinese ancestor cults represent a fixed mode of sanctity. In contrast, Bleeding Host shrines were as devoid of sanctity as they were bereft of identifying features or personality traits.

The correlation between pilgrimage sites devoid of sanctity and a failure to distinguish participatory from observational perceptions of religious ritual—the reason for the all-purpose meaning of *heilig*—is a phenomenon directly contrary to the dynamic of upward displacement recognizable in the history of French pilgrimages. From the outset, Frenchmen traveled to shrines dedicated to *sanctified* personages. No evidence suggests that non-reliquary shrines existed in early medieval France. Later, in the course of time, French pilgrims registered successive advances in the conquest of space by ascribing "higher" hierarchical powers to each set of newly adopted cult objects. At first relics of local saints were supplanted by the bones of ancient martyrs; and this upward displacement of sanctity set in motion a further hierarchization of western Europe's vast collection of relics until the twelfth century. After about 1100, relics located outside Germany and west of the Rhine yielded first to Mary and then to Jesus, celestial personages who, having left no bones and living in no identifiable locations, were therefore conceived to reside in a realm situated outside spatial and temporal processes. The passage from relics of neighborhood thaumaturges to the cult of the Virgin and, finally, in 1215, to the doctrine of transubstantiation—the conversion of the whole substance of the Body and Blood of Christ—diminished the efficacy of relics, and at the same time took the faithful ever further away from their dead. A progressive desacralization of relics—manifested above all by an indifference to being in their proximity—led people to seek less protection from the dead; and, in turn, the dead increasingly assumed the role of grateful supplicants for the prayers of the living. Only some process of upward displacement can create a common dead. The cross-cultural character of this dynamic explains why upward displacement is a major feature in the religious history of every society with a common dead.

Finally, by way of contrast, consider a few phenomena associated with fixed forms of sanctity. In medieval Bavaria and South Germany miracle-working images and other cult objects lost their efficacy when moved from the places where they "belonged." Even German witches lost their power when lifted off the ground. A virtual absence of indigenous sanctity separated German Catholics and German Protestants from their coreligionists on the other side of the Rhine. In Bavaria, in South Germany, and to a lesser extent in other Catholic regions and in several Protestant areas, the fixing of sanctity in particular places seems to have been a necessary part of making certain categories of human beings the source of both religious and social contamination. Jews, gypsies, shepherds, renders, flayers, knackers, millers, itinerant entertainers, executioners, prostitutes, tanners, watchmen, bath attendants, street cleaners, beggars, several categories of textile workers, and (to use the nomenclature then employed) *Sonstige Personen*—"other [undesignated] persons"—were all deemed to be polluted. To eat or drink with such an individual, sometimes even to handle unintentionally the tools of a "contemptible trade," defiled an honorable person. Even contact with a shameful person's shadow was dangerous.

The stigma of "defiled trades" descended to children and grandchildren. They also carried the penalties imposed on people born out of wedlock. Just as "bastards" were said to descend from "no one" so fiends, succubae, and other "unclean spirits" with whom witches are friendly also claimed neither father nor mother. In the sixteenth and seventeenth centuries, when the number of "contemptible occupations" *(Unehrlige Gewerbe)* had reached a maximum—requiring three lines of print for their mere specification[53]—Germans hunted down and burned more witches at the stake, including children, than in all the rest of Europe combined.[54] To be sure, witches were executed as agents of demonic pollution south of the Rhine. But their low numbers relative to the thousands executed in Germany—along with the paucity of "defiled trades"—points to correspondingly diminished anxieties about demonic contamination.

Finally, turn to the contrast between Lutheran and Calvinist or reformed doctrines of the Mass. Luther insisted that Christ descends physically to offer his body to each individual, believer or unbeliever, present at the sacramental rite. Of course only the faithful benefit from such a gift. The belief that the body and blood of Christ could be physically or corporally present in the bread and wine on the Eucharistic table was anathema to the Reformed tradition, according to which Christ is not physically present in the Host. Jesus has only one body, located to the right hand of God in heaven; and the congregation celebrates Communion as a single body. As one scholar put it, "while the Pastor administers the Word both to individuals as well as to congregations, the Eucharist was essentially and uniquely corporate worship."[55] Luther's insistence on the corporeal presence of the body and blood of Christ at the Mass allowed him to reject the doctrine that the whole effectiveness of sanctification or blessing resided entirely in God's Word. Anglican views on this matter seem to have varied from one period to another. And it is not clear that other Protestant denominations have always shared Luther's view that sanctity has no place in a world that is an offense to God.

Gender, Language, and Piety in Cross-Cultural Perspective

•◆•

Late Medieval German Beliefs and American Fundamentalism

The italicized adjective in the caption "*Holy* Roman Empire" acquires other significations when it refers to the "*Holy* Bible." This is not the case in German, a language in which *the holy* and *the sacred* "are one and the same." Only a single word *(heilig)* can refer to sanctity, irrespective of the context. As we saw, this linguistic quirk allowed "the domain of authority claimed in Latin by the *sacrum imperium Romanum* to be semantically extended when rendered through German as the "Holy Roman Empire," a construal that exalted German imperial pretensions."[56]

The politicized sanctity ascribed to the late-medieval German Empire is now manifested in the *holiness* that religious Fundamentalists attribute to the installation of framed copies of the Ten Commandments in numerous courthouses in the United States. In a 5–4 decision the U.S. Supreme Court recently ruled (in June 2005) that this practice violates the Constitutional clause that "Congress shall make no law respecting an establishment of religion." But this provision, known as "the establishment clause," does not apply to a painting on the ceiling of the Supreme Court showing Moses holding a copy of the Ten Commandments. This particular portrayal is deemed to have a primarily historical context.

However, today it is not clear if the special status ascribed to the image in the Supreme Court may also apply to any of the statuary and framed replicas of the Ten Commandments recently established in state legislatures and in other public venues. A spate of litigation about these issues has engendered widespread popular controversy. In discussing these matters it is helpful to remember the import of the Eighth Commandment (Deut. 5:8). It explicitly prohibits the making of statuary and framed inscriptions of the precepts God revealed to Moses on Mount Sinai.

Those who want to exclude biblical precepts from legislative processes have views similar to those that Martin Luther expressed in his famous criticism of politicized invocations to God. He argued that to declare an Empire *holy* is tantamount to claiming that pious cobblers can produce Christian shoes. This memorable quip points to a deeper and more important level of analogy. Just as the rise of Lutheranism threatened Catholic states in the German Empire, so a hitherto huge Protestant majority among American citizens has been significantly reduced by the vast numbers of Muslims, Hindus, Buddhists, and other religious minorities entering the United States since the Vietnam War. Another threat to the Christian Right, an indigenous secularism, is historically represented by Thomas Jefferson, author of the Declaration of Independence. Even as late as 1822 Jefferson continued "to predict that everyone in America would soon become a Unitarian."[57]

The American Revolution introduced the idea that the people were sovereign. But in response to a rapidly growing population of non-Christians, Fundamentalists now seek to limit the freedom of religious preference guaranteed by popular sovereignty. Toward this end Fundamentalists have had monuments bearing inscriptions of the Ten Commandments placed in close proximity to displays of the American flag at municipal, state, and federal structures. To nationalize the Ten Commandments would effectively deny equal public rights to citizens standing outside Judeo-Christian traditions. An open contempt for the establishment clause—compounded by an undisguised abridgement of a right to religious preference—has significantly strengthened movements opposed to Fundamentalist programs.

Religious Immediacy in the United States and in Late Medieval Germany

To suppress abortions, to ban contraceptives, and to prohibit same-sex marriages, Fundamentalists invoke the same biblical authority called upon by witch hunters in late medieval and early modern Germany. Fundamentalism derives its name from

> "The Fundamentals," twelve paperback books issued between 1910 and 1915, edited by A.C. Dixon, which received enormous circulation in the United States. Written by conservative American and British writers, these books constituted a frontal assault upon religious modernism: the doctrines of religious liberalism that asserted an almost perfect congruence between God's will and the inevitable progress of civilization in the United States.[58]

A predominance of Calvinism in early America largely explains why "much of the American religious heritage was a culture shaped by the Old Testament and by Jewish Scriptures."[59] John Calvin "understood the redemptive message to be the same in both the Old and the New Testament."[60] The religious immanence Fundamentalists ascribe to politicizing the Ten Commandments is rooted in a believed intimacy between the Old Testament and the New Testament. Both the content of religious belief and the percentage of "true believers" vary in time and space. But religious belief itself has unchanging traits; and one of them, the immanence and immediacy ascribed to supernatural powers, is as prominent today as it was in the historical past. Although the character of subjectivity and notions of self change, they are nevertheless also affected by the permanent features of religious belief. This section compares forms of religious immediacy in late medieval Germany with those present among American Fundamentalists today.

Late Medieval Germany

Begin with three sets of facts. First, a widespread veneration of Saint Anne, Mary's Mother, took place in Northern Europe between 1480 and 1530. Second, Saint Anne is not a biblical figure. Third, Saint Anne's amazing popularity inspired artists and writers to make a variety of images and to draft diverse descriptions of her person and life. In a remarkable book, Virginia Nixon describes how these writings and images gave

> ...Anne not one but three husbands, and not one but three daughters, all named Mary. Anne's daughters produced a formidable progeny which included along with the Savior, five apostles and a disciple, plus John the Baptist and the early Rhineland bishops Servatius and Maternus. Sculptors, painters, and printmakers in Germany, Flanders, and Holland depicted these family groupings, whether the larger Holy Kinship group or Saint Anne holding Mary and Jesus, with the realism and luxuriance that marked the genius of late Gothic art in the fifteenth and early sixteenth centuries.[61]

The first pilgrimage shrines possessing images and relics of Saint Anne, appearing from about 800 to circa 1350, were highly localized. And the motifs varied. For example, in Brittany Anne's protection of a hero in battle justifies an ecclesiastical claim to a particular piece of territory. After 1300 Anne acquires more generalized functions—such as protecting maritime traffic throughout coastal areas. Virtually all of the twenty-two Anne brotherhoods in existence prior to the 1470s were associated with maritime occupations, on or near the North Sea coast and on rivers suitable for shipping.[62]

Cult images known as *Anna Selbdritt*—where Anne is seen together with Mary and Jesus—reveal that the "Holy Kinship" gradually advanced in social status from the fourteenth to the early sixteenth century. By the fifteenth century "Anne acquired the body type, face, and costume of a mature married woman of the upper levels of the middle class." Subsequently, in the late fifteenth and early sixteenth century, even more distinguished vestments are "displayed to splendid effect in paintings that achieved popularity all over Germany and Flanders."[63]

Although cults to the Holy Kinship flourished in the Netherlands, the Rhineland, England, and France from 1470 to 1530, only Germans showed a widespread tendency to conflate these images with what they represented. People everywhere ascribed an automatic power to proper ritual performance. But toward the end of the fifteenth century, explains Virginia Nixon, "this perception of the relationships between the material and heavenly realms ... operated with particular vigor and persistence in Germany."[64] Luther made the Bible, not images, the source of divine power. In contrast, Calvin's

> ...sense of God's power over the world found formal expression in his doctrine of providence.... "There is no erratic power or action in creatures," he wrote, "but they are governed by God's secret plan in such a way that nothing happens except what is knowingly and willingly decreed by him." God "sustains the world by his energy, he governs everything, however remote, so that not even a sparrow falls to the ground without his decree."[65]

At present, Calvin's doctrine of providence inspires a Fundamentalist mission to nationalize the Ten Commandments throughout the United States.

CHAPTER 5

·◆·

World Religions, Commerce, and Religious
Itinerants in the Age of Empires

UDDHISM AND CHRISTIANITY APPEARED as the first world religions
in the so-called axial age, the millennium from about 500 BCE to
about 500 CE. Buddhism's earliest historical period corresponds roughly
with the reign of Cyrus II, the Great, of Persia (553–529 BCE), founder of the
first world empire. He is the first among a long list of kings who governed
large empires during the subsequent millennium. The historical Buddha,
Sakyamuni—an epithet meaning "sage of the Sakya clan"—may have lived
most of his life in the years between the reigns of Cyrus and Darius I (522–
486).[1] During these nearly seven decades of dynastic supremacy, the Persian
Achaemenid dynasty founded caravansaries in the oasis towns of Central
Asia, known as the eastern section of the "Silk Road." Several centuries later,
by the time of Jesus, a five-thousand-mile network of caravan routes called
the Silk Road connected China with early imperial Rome.

Emperor Ashoka (c. 272–236 BCE) sponsored Buddhism's first period of
significant expansion. The first king to rule over most of the subcontinent,
Ashoka is also notable for having built the first monasteries in human history (in India); and he was also instrumental in establishing early monastic
communities in the trade centers and oasis towns of Central Asia. A little
more than five centuries separate Ashoka from Constantine (306–337), the
first Christian Emperor. Sakyamuni was a prince, and his royal standing
gave considerable authority to the teachings he and his followers preached
for forty years as they traveled through much of India. In contrast, the

founder of the second world religion, a humble peasant from Galilee, enjoyed little recognition. Jesus's public life lasted only two or three years; and his brief time on Earth fell almost entirely between the death of Herod in 4 BCE, and 30 CE. The disparities in the social origins of Sakyamuni and Jesus and the unequal magnitudes of their missionary careers, probably more than any other factor, explain why, unlike the Christians, early Buddhists believed that the religious and political spheres were inseparable.

The Roman Empire and Christianity came onto the historical scene almost simultaneously, and at a very late moment—nearly five centuries after Ashoka had made Buddhism a trans-regional religion. In the Mediterranean, however, Jesus's crucifixion at Roman hands in the reign of the first Emperor, Augustus (31 BCE–14 CE), set the stage for long periods of division between the Church and political authority. Imperial antagonism toward Christianity continued to fluctuate between latent enmity and active persecution until Constantine's accession. Like Ashoka, Constantine founded an empire on explicitly theological principles. But in the three centuries following Jesus's crucifixion most Christians had divorced religious belief from political loyalty. Just as God had prohibited Moses from entering the Promised Land, so Jesus himself may have annunciated the familiar injunction to "render ... unto Caesar the things that are Caesar's, and to God the things that are God's" (Matthew 22: 20–21).[2]

A similar maxim in the Syriac Church, to be discussed in a moment, appears in *The Gospel of Thomas: The Hidden Sayings of Jesus,* a collection of 114 sayings said to have been recounted by Jesus's twin brother. (In the Syriac Church, Judas Thomas was thought to be Jesus's twin brother, the apostle and founder of the Church of the East.) Written between c. 50 and c. 125, the document—from an ancient library found at Nag Hammadi in Upper Egypt—gives voice to the intensely peripatetic piety that was the chief mark of early Syriac Christianity. Religious itinerancy was common to all sectors of the Silk Road. The ascetics who traveled to mercantile centers in northern Mesopotamia, such as Edessa and Nisibis, located between the Euphrates and the Tigris, were supplemented by their counterparts who journeyed to scores of trading cities extending from urban centers near the Upper Nile to Merv, Samarkand, Turfan, and other commercial entrepôts throughout the eastern sectors of the Silk Road.[3]

For example, in saying 42 Jesus tells the faithful, "Be passersby." The command may also be translated to mean "Be wanderers,"[4] a maxim signifying, among other things, that only monetary obligations governed relations between the Emperor and the faithful. As Thomas put it: "Give Caesar the things [coins bearing the Emperor's likeness and inscription] that are Caesar's, give God the things that are God's, and give me what is mine" (saying 100). "The injunction to *give me what is mine,*' a maxim found only in the Gospel of Thomas, elevates the place of Jesus [above the Emperor]."[5] To "render unto Caesar" was seen as analogous to paying a tariff at a border crossing.

Kings, monks, itinerant holy persons, and traveling merchants all contributed, each in their own way, to transforming Buddhism and Christianity into transnational religions. Together, the two great belief systems helped to transform the sanctified, the memorialized, and the despised or forgotten dead into figures possessing distinctive cultural traits which often varied radically from one region to another. Conflicting teachings and dissimilar, often incompatible burial practices contributed to the rise of Islam in the first half of the seventh century. This new world religion differed fundamentally from Buddhism and Christianity, especially with regard to ascetic institutions. Islam "grew out of a revelation to and through a prophet." As one scholar puts it, "the seed of divine speech germinated, through Muhammad's recitation *(qur'an)* into scripture, known as the Qur'an."[6]

Islam stands in a line of revelation that began with God's self-disclosure to the Hebrews; Abraham is seen as the first Muslim—the first man to submit to God. Subsequently, according to Islamic teachings, the Jews and then the Christians fell away from the truth; and a new and final revelation was communicated to the Arab Muhammad in the form of God's own words, transmitted through the archangel Gabriel. In turn, as Muhammad preached these revelations, traveling from one region to the next, the Lord's words were recorded episodically and ultimately codified in the Qur'an some twenty years after the Prophet's death in 632. Thus

Islam's period of meteoric growth—coming long after the initial establishment of world empires—is notable for both a dearth of monks and a paucity of itinerant religious ascetics.

A widespread disregard for ascetic traditions largely deprived political leadership of religious instruction. Ashoka and Constantine, who knew a great deal about the teachings common to the religions they helped to establish, were instrumental in establishing relatively uniform burial practices. This was not the case among Muslim rulers who, ignoring doctrinal precepts, promoted Islam's expansion with minimal attention to how military conquest affected religious practices. Mortuary rites varied from one region to the next; and, to some extent, even notions of the afterlife escaped universal definition. As Peter Brown put it, "In Islam ... the holy tomb, though of inestimable importance throughout all the regions of the Islamic world, existed always a little to one side of Muslim orthodoxy."[7] Royal indifference to the dead helps to explain why ordinary people in Islam rarely associated their kings with great spiritual leaders.

At issue here is the contrast between the *fixity* of Islamic tombs as opposed to the immensely *portable* gift-giving functions of Christian relic translations in late Antiquity. At that time, explains Peter Brown, "the holy" was brought ever closer "through gestures of concord and gift-giving which the men of late antiquity and the early middle ages treasured as the cement of their social world." Social bonds created by frequent relic translations also gave relics "a major place in Christian piety." If this had not happened,

> the spiritual landscape of the Christian Mediterranean might ... have resembled that of the later Islamic world: the holy might have been permanently localized in a few privileged areas, such as the Holy Land, and in "cities of the saints," such as Rome. There might have been a Christian Mecca or a Christian Kerbela, but not the decisive spread of the cult of major saints, such as Peter and Paul, far beyond the ancient frontiers of the Roman world, as happened in Europe of the dark ages. Elsewhere, the holy might have been tied to particularity of local graves.... By

the early fifth century, the strictly "geographical" map of the availability of the holy ... had come to be irreversibly modified by a web of new cult sites, established by the translation of relics, which reflected the dependence of communities scattered all over Italy, Gaul, Spain, and Africa on the enterprise and generosity of a remarkable generation of distant friends.[8]

The close relation of commerce and religion in the early centuries of Buddhism and Christianity went hand in hand with both the immense portability of relic translations and the importance of relics in the formation of a common dead in the two earliest world religions. This reference to large numbers of traveling ascetics on the trade routes draws attention, once again, to the 114 sayings entitled *The Gospel of Thomas: The Hidden Sayings of Jesus,* probably written at the end of the first century. The title has two parts: (1) *The Gospel of Thomas,* and (2) *The Hidden Sayings of Jesus.* The Thomas tradition—which developed over several centuries— begins with The Gospel itself. As mentioned earlier, this text represents the teachings of the early Syriac-speaking Christianity as it was understood in the trade centers that extended from the Upper Nile to Northern Mesopotamia and India.

In contrast, *The Hidden Sayings*—the 114 instructions presented as a dialogue between Jesus and Thomas—have a primarily spiritual content. They describe how to acquire an intimate acquaintance with God by means of an itinerant life. Jesus begins by telling the faithful that the sayings *are* eternal life (saying 1). But only "passersby," travelers without kith, are saved. Redemption is achieved in the course of a wandering existence: "There are many standing at the door, but [only] those who are alone [*monachoi,* the solitary or 'lonely ones'] will enter the wedding chamber" (saying 75).[9] In the late first century—the date of this document—the term *monachos* could not have referred to a monk. A religious itinerant was the first meaning ascribed to the term "monk" *(monachos).* Monastic Christian monks did not exist until Pachomius (c. 290–346) founded a monastic settlement near Nag Hammadi, on the Upper Nile, some two centuries after the *Gospel of Thomas* and about five hundred years after

Ashoka had built the first monasteries. In the Mediterranean, the absence of imperial support for Pachomius's community, and Constantine's general lack of interest in matters concerning coenobitic monasticism—an indifference inherited from an earlier Roman anti-Christian enmity—explain why the Christian monastery never acquired the institutional importance enjoyed by Buddhist cloisters.

The profound differences between Buddhist and early Christian concepts of religious asceticism help to explain why, more than any other institution, it was the monastery that represented Buddhism—first in India and Central Asia, and then throughout Asia. Buddhism began with monks; and after Ashoka's demise it was monasticism, *not* merely an empire, that ensured both the religion's continuity and its subsequent expansion to East Asia. Conversely, bishops, being the highest order of ministers in Christianity, embodied the unity of the church and represented its institutions. Unlike monks, bishops were engaged in the world. But the *Gospel of Thomas* is a pre-monastic document; and it pertained to religious figures, largely wandering ascetics, who escaped episcopal control throughout the pre-monastic period. Only later, more than three centuries after the *Gospel of Thomas,* did the advent of Pachomius's monasteries make it possible for bishops even to think of integrating sedentary ascetics into the ecclesiastical structure.

Death, Holiness, and Relics in the Three World Religions [10]

Individuals known to be intimate with the divine are called *holy*. As mentioned earlier, in English the term *holy* is distinguished from *sacred,* and the distinction is important. Originally a past participle of a now-archaic verb *sacren,* meaning to consecrate, *sacred* may be used to describe human veneration; whereas *holy* often refers to an object or a person hallowed by God. A pious Christian who refers to the "*sacred* books of the East" will call the Bible *holy.* Often the meanings ascribed to these two terms will vary from one context to another.

For example, the enormous popularity of relic cults in antiquity and throughout the Middle Ages led Christians to associate holiness with death. A Christian martyr who conquers death reenacts Christ's paradoxical victory on the Cross in anticipation of a bodily resurrection: "O death, where is thy sting? O, grave, where is thy victory?" (1 Cor. 15:56). Neither the historical Buddha nor Muhammad was a martyr. Yet the Buddha, like Christ, also overcame death. But this was not the case for Muhammad; and relic cults had only a minor importance in Sunni Islam; the sanctity ascribed to Sufi graves is an important exception and will be discussed in a later section. Each world religion has a unique attitude to the body; and in every case it is the founder who defined the body's relation to holiness.

References to the three bodies of the historic Buddha (c. 543–586 BCE) tell us a great deal about the origins of *disembodied* relics. The Buddha "left no writings; it is not even certain that he was literate."[11] His teachings were not written down until near the turn of the millennium. Yet his authority was so great that works attributed to him have been composed in many languages and in many lands over many centuries. The distribution of Gautama's bodily remains at his death set the stage for early Buddhist relic worship. By the third century BCE the Mauryan emperor Ashoka had built hundreds, perhaps thousands of stupas (burial mounds) containing the Buddha's relics. Pilgrims believed that veneration caused the Buddha's remains to multiply, while a decline of pilgrims would lead his relics to shrink and gradually disappear. Worship animates the holy person's remains. Miracle stories describe the Buddha's past activities; and to reinforce their personal faith pilgrims projected these supernatural events into the present. Thus the "life" instantiated by the faithful has both a collective and an individual orientation: one, turned toward the past, seeks the welfare of departed souls; the other looks forward to a devotee's own personal postmortem deliverance.

Reciprocity also governs relations with the personage entombed at the shrine. Even in folk Daoism a god's power (his *ling*) lies with patronage—a forgotten god is a disempowered deity. Only pilgrims can instantiate the sanctity ascribed to the deceased—for, as we saw, without pilgrims the

Buddha's relics shrink and disappear. Also ritual devotion ascribes intermediary functions to the entombed personage. In sum, a multitude of reliquary shrines united living and departed souls into a community that persisted through time.

In Ashoka's reign pilgrimage sanctified the rise of voluntary associations, a movement directly opposed to the Vedic enumeration of priestly, ruling, mercantile, and servant castes. Yet Buddhists accepted in modified form the Vedic doctrine of karma, a system of rewards and punishments attached to one's actions over multiple lifetimes. Buddhists see redemption as a release *(moksha)* from reincarnation. In contrast, Christians believed that God himself lived out a human life in Jesus of Nazareth. The Hebrew Bible says, "God created [both male and female] in his own image" (Gen. 1:27). But the imagehood of God in the human being, as described in Genesis, offers no *theological* message. God's incarnation in Jesus does, however, equate redemption with a *bodily* resurrection.

This uniquely Christian belief stands in opposition to the Buddhist *generic* view of the body. This is why a doctrinal belief in the three bodies of the Buddha (the *Trikaya*) cannot be equated with the Christian Trinity. Buddhists saw life as an event in a beginning-less cycle of birth, death, and rebirth, occurring in the realms of gods, demigods, humans, animals, ghosts, and hell beings. This panoramic view of the body is also expressed in sacred writings known as "dharma relics"—alphabetical formulae with no lexical meaning (called *mantras* and *dharanis*)—that were inserted, along with sutras, in stupas and sacred images at the time scripture was disseminated throughout Asia, from about 100 BCE to 100 CE. To help the faithful escape reincarnation Buddhists abolished animal sacrifice and made desire the source of karmic consequences. Since desire is common to all human beings, it is a faculty consistent with a generic view of the human body. And dharma relics, especially mantras, offer a language free of desire. They are written words representing sacred sounds which, having no lexical meaning, were often understood to be the literal words or sounds of the Buddha.

Mantras—originally sung in Vedic religion to invoke the gods during sacrificial rituals—had several uses. Not only were they inserted, sometimes along with sutras, in stupas and images, but people throughout Buddhist Asia also chanted these formulae in tantric rituals. In sum, mantras supplanted the Buddha's bodily relics; and incantations such as OM MANI PADME HUM (an invocation of the bodhisattva Avalokitesvera) expressed on a popular plane the Buddhist ideal of holiness or *nirvana* (a "blowing out"). The point to stress is that these ritual words without lexical meaning were thought to be indescribable in the same sense that a cessation of craving is indescribable. In sum, dharma relics preserved essential aspects of Indian oral traditions at a time when vast collections of Buddhist scriptures were first disseminated throughout Asia.

Turn once again to the fact that kings, monks, wandering holy people, and traveling merchants—major figures in the rise of Buddhism and Christianity—all contributed in different ways to ascribe distinctive cultural traits to the sanctified, the memorialized, and the despised or forgotten dead. A somewhat comparable process took place in Islam. But conflicting teachings and dissimilar, often incompatible burial practices associated with the rise of Islam made cultural fusion much more difficult to attain in the first half of the seventh century, a time when religious expansion was prodigious. In a mere century after the death of Muhammad (570–632), Islam had reached the Atlantic in one direction and the borders of China in the other. At present the religion counts about a billion adherents, with followers in most countries of the world. Islam's diffusion may be likened to a flow of water over ground in the sense that the cult tends to take on the ideological hues of the regions of the Earth it happens to engulf.

Mortuary practices varied locally; and in some ways even the afterlife escaped a uniform definition. Perhaps as a result, Sunni orthodox theology has always been rather wary of the tombs of Sufi holy people. The relative paucity of Islamic relic cults may be partly attributed to the fact that Islamic religious experience largely came out of conflict with other monotheistic religions. The slow development of saints' shrines in Islam— except for the thousands of pilgrims who visited the tomb-shrines of Sufi saints, a topic to be discussed shortly—may also be ascribed to a failure to draw a clear distinction between spiritual and temporal realms. Like other societies suffering from ambivalent relations to the dead, Islamic culture is obsessed with purity. All creatures and things are perceived to be inherently pure or polluted. The dynamic leading people to equate purity with either an idea of sanctity or even with a concept of holiness, while identifying defilement with evil, needs to be discussed in both a cross-cultural and historical context. Toward this end, the following section begins by examining concepts of holiness and defilement in the Hebrew Bible. Then a scriptural explanation is proposed for why the terms *holy* and *sacred* function as an analogue to *purity* and *defilement*. Later sections describe how this paired polarity operates in widely separated religious and cultural environments: in Islam and in ancient Greece. Finally, chapter 6 discusses how Silk Road religions contributed to the rise of world religions.

Purity, Defilement, Temples, and Burials in the Hebrew Bible, the Ancient Mediterranean, and Islam

Christian tradition depicts Satan as the archenemy of God, the personification of evil. In contrast, the term "Satan" has several designations in the Hebrew Bible. For example, "Satan" referred to any human being who played the role of an accuser. Also, among several other alternative meanings, "Satan" alluded to beings associated with the verb "to rove," as in the following passage from *The Book of Job:*

> Now there was a day when the sons of God came to present themselves before the Lord, and Satan came among them. The Lord said to Satan, "Whence have you come?" Satan answered the Lord, "From going to and fro on the earth, and walking up and down on it" (1:6–7).

The passage is repeated, word for word, a few paragraphs later (Job 2:3). And in both instances, Satan warns God against extending a helping hand to Job, who "will curse thee to thy face" (1:11 and 2:5). The Hebrew God clearly represents a fixed form of sanctity. A ritual avoidance of portable modes of sanctity explains why the Lord curses Satan for "going to and fro on the earth, and walking up and down on it."

Moreover, Hebrew notions of ritual purity are consistent with fixed forms of sanctity. A distinguished anthropologist, Mary Douglas, argues that in ancient Israel ritual impurities involved various forms of disorder such as "whoring after other gods" and uncontrolled bodily emissions. But contact with a dead body and the dwelling place of the dead, Sheol or Hades, were viewed as the ultimate sources of contamination. God's people "shall not defile themselves by going near a dead person" (Ezekiel 45:25). The word "Sheol," found sixty-five times in the Hebrew Bible, refers both to death itself and also to the realms of death beneath the earth. For example, toward the end of his life Samuel, Israel's leader in the transition from the premonarchic to the monarchic period, complained that

> the waves of death encompassed me, the torrents of perdition assailed me; the cords of Sheol entangled me, the snares of death confronted me (2 Samuel 22:5-6).

Return for a moment to an earlier discussion about Ezekiel, a biblical prophet who was among the Jews exiled to Babylonia in 607 BCE In chapter 3, the section entitled "Avoidance of Corpse Defilement: Double Burial and the Rise of World Religions" cites passages from a famous chapter (Ezekiel 37) in which the prophet describes how God assisted him with having Jews in the Dispersion disinter the dead and arrange for their reburial in Palestine. By equating redemption with a common afterlife, achieved by burial of deceased Jews in the Dispersion, Ezekiel has God transform Palestine into a Holy Land. This early description of a resurrection prepared the ground, as it were, for the eventual advent of Jesus six centuries later.

In a contrary message, God protests to Ezekiel against the prevailing practice of burying Jewish kings in the restored temple. God addresses the prophet, declaring that the new temple

> is the place of my throne and the place of the soles of my feet, where I will dwell in the midst of the people of Israel forever. And the house of Israel shall no more defile my holy name, neither by their harlotry and by the dead bodies [or monuments] of their kings, by setting their threshold by my threshold and

their doorposts by my doorposts, with only a wall between me and them. They have *defiled* my *holy* name by their abominations ... so I have consumed them in my anger. Now let them put away their idolatry and the dead bodies [or monuments] of their kings far away from me, and I will dwell in their midst forever [43:7–9; italics added].

An implicit contradiction is embedded in these lines. The defilement attributed to the placement of royal funerary monuments in the restored sanctuary is an accusation that conflicts with the redemptive qualities Ezekiel (in chapter 37) ascribed to the reburial of exiled Jews in Palestine. God explicitly promised to *resurrect* the dead who were disinterred and then reburied in the Holy Land: "Thus says the Lord God: Behold I will open your graves, and raise you from your graves, O my people; and I will bring you home into the land of Israel" (Ezekiel 37:12). If, as the prophet declared, reburial of displaced Jews in their land of origin resurrects the dead and also transforms Palestine into a holy land, it follows that Ezekiel, however unwittingly, had also announced that God transferred the holiness ascribed to the temple to all of Palestine.

How New Meanings Were Ascribed to "Holy" and "Sacred"

Before the destruction of the Temple (598/97 BCE) and Ezekiel's deportation to Babylon (607 BCE) in the company of other Judeans, God resided in the Temple; and there were two kinds of death. A natural death was accompanied by unification with kin—much as in ancient China—and the realm of the dead, Sheol, is never mentioned in connection with the death of a family member. Only the wicked—such as the Prince of Tyre who "sat in the seat of the gods"—are condemned to lie with the uncircumcised in "the Pit." Consider, for example, the following passage from Ezekiel (28:6–10):

Thus says the Lord God: "Because you consider yourself as wise as a god ... I will bring strangers upon you, the most terrible of the nations; and they shall draw their swords against the beauty of your wisdom and defile your splendor. They shall thrust you down into the Pit, and you shall die the death of the slain in the heart of the seas. Will you still say, 'I am a god' in the presence of those who slay you? You shall die the death of the uncircumcised by the hand of foreigners; for I have spoken," says the Lord God.

Later, when Ezekiel reformed burial practices so as to have Jews who died in the Dispersion be disinterred and reburied in Palestine, all the deceased were treated as members of a single family. Sheol disappeared when Ezekiel equated a nationalized dead with a resurrection; and God transferred his holiness from the restored temple to all of Israel. But the temple Ezekiel describes (chapters 40–48) points to an ideal, not to an existing sanctuary. As one scholar puts it, Ezekiel's temple "is presented as a vision, and so the details may be assumed to be symbolic rather than material."[12]

To portray the restored temple as a symbol and to declare the reburial of displaced Jews in their country of origin transforms Palestine into a holy land was also to proclaim a common dead and to make the public sphere responsible for the regulation of funerary services. People no longer buried the dead with their kin.

Moreover, the formation of a common dead and an incipient foundation for a public sphere contributed, however distantly, to the popular support subsequently shown for the worship of a charismatic person such as Jesus. Consider, for example, the contrast between the manifest failings and corruption associated with the Temple in the time of Jesus and Ezekiel's vision of an exemplary house of God. The comparison probably inspired the passage in the second Gospel where Jesus proclaims the eventual and eschatological destruction of the Temple. It is difficult to imagine another source for the prophetic announcement ascribed to Jesus in Gospel of Mark:

And as he came out of the temple, one of his disciples said to him, "Look, Teacher, what wonderful stones and what wonderful buildings!" And Jesus said to him, "Do you see these great buildings? There will not be left here one stone upon another, that will not be thrown down" (Mark 13:1–2).

Social Death and the Meaning of Asceticism

In the two earliest world religions holy persons were perceived to be religious elites who voluntarily suffered a social death. As mentioned earlier, the Buddha and his followers, much like Jesus and his disciples five hundred years later, were itinerant ascetics. An ascetic devoted to Sakyamuni or to Jesus was, as Peter Brown put it, "a man who had made himself 'dead.' But the death was a *social* death, and did not follow from a mortification of the body" (italics added).[13] Much the same principle applies to Muslim ascetics. Muslims defined themselves as members of *Dar al-Islam,* the "house of Islam" or, alternatively, "house of submission [to God]." Scholars known as the *ulama* were learned guardians of the divinely created law *(shari'a).* They were trained in schools called *madrasas,* which were usually founded by rulers and often attached to mosques. As an institution associated with the study of law, the mosque is a temple which has few spiritual functions and does not provide for rituals to be performed for the dead.

Islamic piety is represented by charismatic and largely itinerant holy persons called sufis. Probably more influential than the *ulama,* sufis popularized *Sufism,* an Islamic mysticism. Ordinary people believed that sufi holy men (and a few women) enjoyed a special closeness to God. These itinerant ascetics embraced social death so as to enjoy a union with God. Conversely, *ulamas,* the guardians of divine law, had a deeply social function. The division is profound. Thousands of followers listened to the sermons of the greatest sufi mystics. And orders of sufi "brotherhoods" established after the death of these famous leaders preserved their teachings for centuries. Muslims believed that a holy person was a "friend of God" *(wali)*—a title which, as we shall soon see, was first ascribed to kings and heroes in the age following Alexander (the Great) of Macedon (337–323 BCE). In Islam, a friend of God often acted as an advocate for the less religious bulk of the population both in life and after death. Thousands of pilgrims visited the tombs of deceased *walis;* and their grave sites are the source of many legends about the inspired teachings and miraculous exploits associated with their names.[14]

Types of Temples and Modes of Sanctity:
A Cross-Cultural Perspective

In Antiquity and in the Middle Ages Christian churches were placed in cemeteries. Conversely, Jews, Muslims, and ancient Greeks protected their temples against the defilement thought to emanate from tombs. In ancient Greece people believed that the gods resolutely averted their eyes from death. A play by Euripides describes how Hippolytus enjoyed an unusual intimacy with the goddess Artemis. But when Hippolytus lay dying, Artemis banished him from her sight, declaring: "And now farewell! T'is not for me to gaze upon the dead, or to pollute my sight with death scenes."[15] Occasionally, Greeks found it difficult to keep burial places far enough away from temples to avoid polluting the eyes of the gods. Herodotus tells us that in 546 BCE Pisistratus, the tyrant of Athens (who allegedly descended from the deity Neleus), decided to "cleanse the island of Delos." He ordered that "all the dead bodies that were buried within the sight of the temple be dug up and reinterred in another part of the island" (Bk. I, 62–65). More than a century later, in 426 BCE, adverse fortunes in the Peloponnesian War (431–404) prompted the Athenian statesman Nicias to take more stringent measures to purify Delos. In the winter of 426, explains Thucydides (III, 8),

> The Athenians no doubt because of some Oracle, carried out ceremonies of purification on Delos. In former times the tyrant Pisistratus also purified the island, though not as much as could be seen from the temple. On the present occasion, however, the whole island was purified in the following way. All the tombs of those who had died on Delos were dug up, and it was proclaimed that [in the future] no deaths or births were to be allowed on Delos. Those who were about to die or to give birth were to be carried across to Rhenea.

During the 120 years separating the two purifications of Delos—mythical home of Apollo and Artemis—Greeks built substantial numbers of incubation temples, centers for ritually induced sleep to obtain a dream, usually for healing. Most of them were dedicated to Apollo's son, Asclepius. The earliest signs of belief in a new post-mortem destiny may have taken place when Athenians showed great concern to protect the island's sanctity during Athens' leadership of the Delian League (478/77). At that time small numbers of deceased souls, known as the *psychai* of the dead, started traveling toward the heavens.[16] Reports of these celestial ascents appear when many people entered newly built incubation temples seeking cures from sickness in a ritually induced sleep.

In the early fifth century concerns about the *(psychai)* of the dead and the therapeutic dreams acquired in incubation temples—which seem to have had much in common with the prominence of dreams in early Athenian tragedy—took place in the period when successive purifications of Delos had established a system of double burial. At this time, visual contact with the divine—usually accomplished in the ritual viewing of cult images and dream images—was among the supreme religious ideals in ancient Greece. A perceived relation between temples built for cult images and incubation temples is suggested by the reference to *"pleasant sleep"* in the following sentence uttered by a viewer upon seeing a statue built by Phidias, a famous Athenian sculptor who was active from c. 465 to 425 BCE:

> I think that a man full of weariness in his soul,
> who has suffered from many misfortunes and
> pains and cannot even find pleasant sleep, if he
> stood suddenly in front of this image, would
> forget all the awful and grievous things to be
> experienced in this life.[17]

In sum, sanctifying powers resided in the *silent* viewing of a cult image or a dream-image. No sanctity was ascribed to dreams recounted by actors in a theatrical play. In such instances the audience could only *hear* about a dream no one had *seen*.[18] As one scholar puts it, "Homer's dreams were both visual and linguistic events."[19]

•◆•

Astonishing cross-cultural parallels have repeatedly appeared throughout this volume. For example, in ancient Israel, ancient Greece, and medieval Japan we see: (1) double burials; (2) possession of a common dead; (3) political centralization; and (4) the formation of a public sphere. Dream figures on the theatrical stage, however, appear only in ancient Greece and in early modern Japan. But, apart from this exception, widespread pilgrimage and numerous temples appear in all three societies.[20] Also, new information about Japanese double burial raises an unexpected chronological consideration. Mark Blum, a friend and colleague in Japanese Buddhism, tells me that double burials—some designed for cremation and others for interment—are as common in present-day Japan as they were in the medieval period.[21] Without portable modes of sanctity and possession of a common dead—elements essential to the formation of a public sphere—no society can achieve cultural integration.

Friends of Gods, Upward Displacement, and the Rise of Empires

Ancient Greeks referred to distant peoples who seemed to share cultural affinities with their own society as occupants of an oecumene *(oikumene)*. The term denoted "the world," a realm inhabited "by peoples seen as relevantly similar."[22] The concept goes back to about 300 BCE—when at least one third of city-state-dwelling Greeks resided in city-states founded after 700 BCE. From about 734 to 580 religion and colonization were united in an Athenian personage chosen to be the founder or *oikist*—the leader, supreme organizer, and military commander of a newly established colony. Only an oracle could commission an *oikist*. Toward this end, the postulant visited an oracle at one of the four great pan-Hellenic sanctuaries, usually Delphi,[23] where he accepted a personal designation as *oikist* and received a divinely inspired command to colonize. "The journey, the choice of the actual site, relations (and wars) with natives, division and allocations of sacred lands, the performing of proper rites, and the establishing of cults" were all responsibilities assumed by the founder.[24]

Once invested with religious authority, the *oikist* and the colonists gathered at the public dining room *(prytaneion)*—the symbolic center of the city—which housed the communal hearth containing the eternal flame. To establish a colony Greeks gathered "seeds of flame" from the common hearth, put them in earthen pots, and carried the sacred fire to mark the founding of a new settlement.[25] The sacred fire helped to found altars and precincts; and, most important, the "seeds of flame" attached new colonies to Athens. The illustrious Mother City also produced many heroes. Athenian *oikists* who had died in the many cities they founded were not only recognized as heroes, but the sacred fire consecrating these heroes transferred their fame to Athens. The Mother City had numerous children; and many urban centers helped to internationalize Greek hero cults by colonial expansion. Indeed, "it is no exaggeration to say that by 580 [BCE] all the most obvious areas in the then available world had been occupied to at least some extent by Greeks.[26]

The classical polis was a city built around a common space, the market square or agora. A local hero's grave—known as a *heroon*—marked the center of the public square. Debates about matters of public concern took place in the presence of the interred hero. Citizens also had a duty to sit in the court of law, and to participate in decisions for common action. Speech revealed and made "all things visible"[27] to both the living and the dead. The presence of entombed heroes at the center of political life in Greek cities, representing a common dead, helped to transform a multitude of market squares into a "free" or "public" realm.

Hero graves honored with a cult go back to the eighth century BCE. From this time onwards, explains Walter Burkert, a distinguished specialist of ancient Greek religion, the worship of heroes "must be...derived directly from the influence of epic poetry." The rise

> of the hero cult under the influence of epic poetry has its significance and its function in the evolution of the Greek polis; the prominence given to the [hero's] specific grave goes hand in hand with the suppression of the customary cult of the dead....

> The hero cult…is not an ancestor cult; its concern is with the effective presence, not with the chain of blood across generations…. Hand in hand with the rise of the hero cult goes a restructuring in spiritual life [expressed above all] in the radical separation of the realm of the gods from the realm of the dead, of the Olympian from the Chthonic. Whoever has died is not a god; whoever is honored as dwelling in his grave … must have been a mortal—preferably of course, a mortal from that greater, earlier [legendary] age. The gods are elevated as an exclusive group into an ideal Olympus; whatever is left behind is subsumed under the category of demigods.[28]

Just as the polis recognized no power superior to the assembled body of male citizens, so Zeus—the only political God among the Olympians—had no marks of kingship. Nor did images of rulers appear on coins minted in Greek cities. Royal visages appear on coins, both in profile and in full face, only after the death of Alexander, "the Great," of Macedon in 323 BCE. The date marks the beginning of a new era. The three centuries between Alexander's demise and 31 BCE—the year Octavian (later Augustus, the first Roman Emperor) defeated Marcus Antonius Actium—are known as the Hellenistic Age. At this time inscriptions such as "Savior" *(Soter)* or "Benefactor" *(Evergetes)* appeared beneath the sovereign face imprinted on the coin.

These words had a wide range of meanings. *Soter* could refer to gods or to men. When applied to the latter, however, the term did not necessarily suggest that such men either belonged or were even approximated to the category of gods. In general, therefore, *soter* denoted a performance of a function, not membership or position in a hierarchy of beings. In contrast,

> *Evergetes,* although also applicable to gods and heroes, is a word which clearly has its roots in the human arena. In classical times and thereafter it was a regular term in civic degrees to denote a man whose name was thus to be set on stone and recorded as one of the city's benefactors … in Hellenistic times

the category of *evergetai* received the honor of public sacrifices or games. This involved the putting into practice of a principle … that honors such as were paid to divinity were the highest expression of gratitude.[29]

In the Hellenistic Age coins led most people to believe that kings were "friends of the gods."

Alexander ("the Great") of Macedon (356–323), probably more than any other royal personage, helped to popularize terms such as *soter* and *evergetes,* contributing thereby to the belief that great kings and high officials were "friends of the gods." The process whereby divine attributes were ascribed to monarchs begins with the image of Heracles stamped on coins minted during Alexander's reign. Macedonian kings traced their descent back to Heracles (Heroditus, 8, p. 135; Thucydides, 2, p. 99). As Walter Burkert points out, "there is no grave of Heracles, and just as the stories about him are known everywhere, so his cult extends through the entire Greek world and far beyond. Heracles is therefore both a hero and a god." Two qualities contributed to the widespread acceptance of Heracles' spiritual qualities. As Walter Burkert puts it,

> First, he is the prototype of the ruler who by virtue of his Divine legitimation acts in an irresistible way for the good of mankind and finds his fulfillment among the gods. Secondly, he is a model for the common man who may hope that after a life of drudgery, and through that very life, he too may enter into the company of the gods.[30]

Alexander claimed Heracles as an eponymous ancestor, and the deity's image appeared on his coins. Heracles' image enjoyed a recognition that was roughly commensurate with Alexander's fame; and a widespread tendency to identify Heracles with Alexander led many people to think the Emperor acted for the good of mankind. Although there were no cults to Alexander, his popularity led the Emperor's successors—who divided up the empire among themselves—to place Heracles' image on their coins.

CHAPTER 6

Silk-Road Pieties and the Rise of World Religions

ALEXANDER'S ASTONISHING MILITARY VICTORIES led to a dissemination of Greek culture throughout his empire. The presence of large numbers of Greeks along eastern sections of the Silk Road and in northwest India during Alexander's reign profoundly influenced the history of early Buddhism. Elsewhere, outside of Palestine, Christianity developed among Jewish communities dispersed in North Africa, Babylonia, Persia, and other areas in or near trade centers in western sectors of the Silk Road. Large-scale migrations of Greeks and Jews, attaining new magnitudes toward the second century BCE, contributed to the rise of empires and also to an enormous growth of overland traffic along a five-thousand-mile network of trading centers connecting Rome and China at the turn of the millennium. Itinerant ascetics, representing Gnostics, Elkesaites, Zoroastrians, Manicheans, and numerous other Silk Road religions, followed in the wake of merchants and caravans. This chapter discusses how the efforts of peripatetic holy men to bring local populations in direct contact with the divine helped to transform Buddhism and Christianity into world religions.

Jewish Dispersions and Religious Identity
Among Jewish Peoples Outside Palestine

The dispersion of Jews throughout the ancient world began with the Assyrian invasion of Palestine in 722 BCE, and an ensuing deportation of the entire population of the northern kingdom, called Israel. A second exile, this time to Babylonia, came in the wake of Nebuchadnezzar's conquest of Judea and the destruction of the first Temple in 587 BCE. Unlike Assyria's suppression and dissolution of Israel, Babylon's invasion of Judea did not lead to the disappearance of its people. Only the upper classes were deported. Subsequently, a small number of their descendants, around a thousand males, emigrated to Palestine in 539—following the fall of Babylonia in 539 BCE to Cyrus (II), "the Great," founder of the Persian (Achaemenid) Empire. At this time, fifty years after Nebuchadnezzar's entry into Palestine, few of the original Jewish deportees were alive. Why did some of their descendants leave their homes in Babylon to rebuild a Temple and establish civil institutions in a land they had never seen?

The behavior was unusual, to say the least. Many peoples suffered exile in the ancient world; and their descendants built their temples in the lands where they resided. Only Jews insisted on restoring houses of worship at their original historical sites. This singular practice was inspired by the central event recounted in the Hebrew Bible: an original escape from slavery in Egypt and a subsequent entry into the Promised Land under Moses's leadership. Most deities, including the Jewish God, were attached to specific territories; and, unlike Yahweh, they showed little concern for ethnicity. This is why few deities in the sixth century BCE demanded a uniformity of religious practices. But after Cyrus the Great of Persia, who conquered Babylon in 539 BCE, issued an edict permitting the descendants of exiled Jews to leave Babylonia and rebuild a temple in the land of their ancestors, the small minority of Jews who emigrated to Palestine acquired a strong sense of their ethnicity. This was not the case for the majority of Jews. And like all Jews "in the diaspora communities that would flourish in the subsequent centuries," explains Shaye J. D. Cohen, they "were willing to forgo even their temple and their land."[1]

For more than a thousand years Jews accepted life under the rule of a series of foreign sovereigns, beginning with the Hellenistic kingdoms of Egypt and Syria. Subsequently, under the Romans, their Christian continuators, and the Parthians, Jews increasingly identified their ethnicity with the Holy Land. Today many Israelis complain that foreign domination and exile has been the plight of Jews from 587 BCE to the founding of the state of Israel in 1948. This view projects modern nationalism into the ancient world. The Holocaust inspired Jews to establish the state of Israel. Few Israelis even know, much less could they care, that some 1,000 *males*,[2] most of them sons and grandsons of deported religious leaders, left home in 538 BCE to rebuild a temple destroyed by the King of Babylon fifty years earlier.

Important demographic facts are at issue here. In the later sixth century BCE the Jewish population count was exceedingly small. "The best modern estimates are that the world's 'Jewish' population was 150,000, mostly in Palestine."[3] Subsequently, in the period of mercantile expansion and the rise of empires, many gentiles adopted the Jewish faith in regions outside Palestine, especially in Syria and Babylon. For example, the large numbers of gentiles who converted to Judaism in the lands extending from Antioch to Adiabene, in the third century BCE, allowed a merchant-convert, Izates, to found a Jewish kingdom called Charax Spasini between the mouths of the Euphrates and Tigris rivers.[4] By the late first century BCE, Jews had become "a major ethnic group in the [Roman] empire, comprising 5 to 7 percent of the empire's population."[5] More than 90 percent of the four to eight million Jews residing in Roman lands during Augustus's reign (31 BCE–14 CE)[6] lived *outside* Palestinian borders.

Centuries of sustained population growth led Jews living in the Dispersion to favor the Greek language over Hebrew. For example, the first versions of the Greek Bible, known as the Septuagint (LXX), appeared in the first century. During the Hellenistic age—the three centuries from Alexander's death in 323 BCE to the dissolution of the Ptolemaic dynasty in Egypt (30 BCE)—most Jews were conversant in Greek, and many could neither read nor speak Hebrew. The Christian Gospels were written in Greek; and educated Jews who adopted Christianity sought solace in the New Testament.

Why "Aniconic Monotheism" Attracted Some Pagans to Judaism in the Time of Saint Paul

John Dominic Crossan, the foremost Jesus scholar of our time, recently joined with Jonathan L. Reed, a distinguished archeologist of first-century Palestine, to write a remarkable work entitled *In Search of Paul: How Jesus's Apostle Opposed Rome's Empire with God's Kingdom, A New Vision of Paul's Words and World.*[7] Of special interest here is their discussion about why some pagans were sufficiently attracted to Judaism to become semi-Jews, called "God-fearers" or "God-worshippers." The authors explain as follows:

> Apart from social, political, economic, or personal reasons, there was one very special factor. Greek and then Roman thinkers appreciated and admired Jewish *aniconic monotheism,* that is, the belief that there was but one transcendent and un-image-able divinity.[8]

Most pagans venerated temple images, and many were deeply offended by Jewish aniconic monotheism. But there was also a third path between Judaism and paganism. An "intermediate way in which people retained the culture of paganism and accepted the faith of Judaism, a middle option for those who believed in Jewish monotheism and its moral law, but did not submit to all its ritual law" nor to circumcision or other "socioreligious markers."[9] In sum, "God-fearers" and "God-worshippers" were not converts; yet they were important to the survival of Judaism. Neither pagan nor Jew, the "worshipping ones"—a Greek term, *sebomai,* meaning "devout"—provided a buffer zone of Jewish sympathizers. They formed islands of protection against frequent pagan hostility to Jews in the Diaspora.

Crossan and Reed argue that Paul, traditionally known as "the Apostle of the Gentiles," must have addressed his letters and sermons to these God-worshippers. Challenging anyone to "pick up any letter of Paul's and read a passage at random," the authors show that "no pure pagan or community of pure pagans could understand what on Earth he was talking about."

Even granting prior oral instruction and conversion to Christ, how could they understand those intensively Jewish arguments, those extensively Jewish concerns. But sympathizers, on the other hand, knew quite a bit about the Jewish religion's traditional faith, scriptural basis, and ritual requirements. With a core of sympathizers in his communities, Paul already had with him those who were neither Jew nor Greek or, better, both Jew and Greek at the same time.

What about the Romans? After all, Paul's longest letter is addressed to the Roman Christians. The authors show that the letters Paul addressed to people in the Roman church were largely received by Gentiles who had "lived as sympathizers on the margins of synagogues before they became Christian."[10]

A wide range of written and archeological evidence shows a continuous oscillation between approval and disapproval when Greeks and Romans discussed Jews and Judaism. On occasions Judaism's great success led many pagans to believe there was a serious chance for the establishment of a Jewish Roman Empire. Paul powerfully contributed to the conversion of Greek and Roman God-worshippers to Christianity. More than any other single factor, the Apostle's systematic estrangement of God-worshippers from Judaism to Christianity set the stage for the ultimate rise of a Christian Empire.

The Odor of Sanctity and the Stench of Sin: Burial Practices on the Silk Road

The history of Greek influence in early Buddhism begins with a text entitled "Milinda's Questions" (a sutra, known as the *Milindapanha*). It takes the form of a record of conversations between the monk Nagasena and Milinda (or Menander), king of Sagala, in Bactrian Greece. The legends of King Milinda—who ruled from 155 to 130 BCE—go back to the second century BCE, to a time shortly after the monarch's death. Much later the stories were collected by Plutarch, a Greek philosopher and biographer (born before 50 CE and died after 120). The earliest portions of this sutra, however, were composed around the time of Jesus, that is, in the early years of the Kushan Empire. In Milinda's reign, Sagala was a major trade center located in the Himalayan foothills somewhere between the Swat valley and the Punjab in Northwest India. Sagala's wealth allegedly rivaled the riches of Uttara-kuru—a mythical metropolis—and "in glory it is as…the city of the gods" (I, 2–3). Sagala's celestial counterpart, the City of Nirvana, was the home of those who have crossed "the ocean of Samsara." This glorious city is

> spotless and stainless, pure and white, ageless and deathless, where all is security and calm and bliss. In the city of Nirvana [one] emancipates his mind in Arhatship! And this, O King is what is called "the Blessed one's bazaar of flowers…. [The] categories of virtue … anointed by the perfume of … righteousness … the fragrant incense and perfume of goodness [pervades the] whole world of gods and men" [V, 6–7].

The previous chapter devoted a few lines to the *Gospel of Thomas: The Hidden Sayings of Jesus,* a collection of 114 sayings said to have been recorded by Jesus's twin brother, the alleged apostle and founder of the Church of the East. The document represents the piety of religious itinerants traveling among mercantile centers extending from the Upper Nile, Syria, and northern Mesopotamia to Merv, Samarkand, Turfan, and other entrepôts in the eastern sectors of the Silk Road.

A brief history of burial practices in some of these regions tells us a lot about the "odor of sanctity" on the Silk Road. Begin with the evolution of burials in Palmyra, an oasis city in the Syrian desert. Allegedly founded by Solomon—and known in the Hebrew Bible as "Tadmor in the wilderness" (2 Chronicles 8:4)—Palmyra was an important caravan city located halfway between the Phoenician coast and the Euphrates, some 300 kilometers south of Edessa, a major Syrian mercantile center. Virtually all overland trade bound for India, Alexandria, and Rome passed through this Arab trading state during the first three centuries of the Common Era. The indigenous language was practically the same as the Jewish Aramaic of the

Dead Sea Scrolls, and very close to Biblical Aramaic. Apart from a tiny chapel to an Arab goddess (c. 50 BCE), all extant monuments were built about the time of Jesus or later. In 17 CE two statues of Emperor Tiberius and his kin were erected in the great temple dedicated to the chief god, Bel, probably a deity of Babylonian origin.

Fifty years later, under Nero (54–68), the caravan city became a major merchant power with outposts in Babylon and Selucia-on-the-Tigris, and later in Vologesias and Charax, river ports near the Persian Gulf. Finally, when Emperor Hadrian visited Palmyra in 129 he made it a free city; and his bestowal of fiscal autonomy contributed to Palmyra's mercantile ascendancy in the generation from 130 to about 160, the period when commercial traffic on the Silk Road attained its highest volume. Among the archeological remains dating from the second and third centuries CE are about two hundred partly preserved tombs found in the necropolis located immediately outside the city. Mortuary towers containing multiple bodies stand above ground; and the same is true for funerary monuments housing only one deceased person or a family.

Conversely, in tombs located beneath the earth, corpses are preserved in vertical niches carved into the walls of long galleries. The upright bodies are presented individually in the same artistic style as the religious images in the city above. Both the gods above ground and the mummified corpses beneath the earth are represented in relief, and aligned in a strictly frontal view. The vividness of the large open eyes among the mummies, along with a corresponding frontal posture presented by the statues of gods, communicates the intimacy that joined the deceased believers to their deities above ground.[11]

Mercantile ascendancy financed the city's elaborate statuary and other mortuary monuments. Palmyra's majestic sepultures exemplify a revolutionary change in the way people buried their dead. The second-century necropolis points to a dramatic discontinuity with whatever burial practices existed in the oasis city in periods before the Common Era. Especially noteworthy is the absence of evidence suggesting that people fed or ate with the dead in the second century. For eating with the dead—a custom going back several centuries before the Common Era—had been an indigenous practice in these regions among both Christians and non-Christians.

Previously, during the first and second centuries, Christians in North Africa and Egypt were notable for food offerings to the dead, on the one hand, and for equating sin with putrefaction, on the other. To maintain an alimentary intimacy with the deceased, the faithful preserved corpses in a purified state. As one scholar put it, North Africa was the

> "bible belt" of the Mediterranean. At once severe and enthusiastic, fundamentalist and traditional in their biblical orientation and proud of their origins as the "church of the martyrs," North African Christians gave to the Latin church its earliest act of the martyrs and the most energetic cult of the saints. They buried their dead in wet plaster to preserve every detail of the body's outline; they could break into a near riot if "ivy" was substituted for "gourd" in a reading from the prophet Jonah during a sermon. The church's experiences in the drastic days of Roman persecutions determined its view both of itself and of the outside world: it was the community of the holy, the ark of salvation sealed against the temptations and tempests of a hostile environment, a permanent option to pagan society.[12]

Only when the corpse was encased in wet plaster and put in a coffin built with apertures for food and libations did Christians in North Africa and Egypt believe that a funeral ceremony had ended. An intimacy with the dead in these regions goes back to the periodic mortuary feasts practiced in a period long before the time of Jesus.

Moreover, Christians residing in lands from Egypt to southern Syria also believed that putrefaction was "bad publicity for God."[13] Their demand for a burial *ad sanctos* went hand in hand with the pre-Christian practice of embalming and "salting down" their dead. The abundance of martyrs was prodigious, especially after the Roman campaigns against North African Christians in 311–312. Persecution intensified the desire to be interred near the body of a saint. In a local cemetery the saints were almost without exception wedged in between a heap of other graves. It was this practice that … caused three quarters of the catacombs to be burrowed out into the labyrinth of corridors which worked their way around the famous graves of an earlier necropolis. The nearer one comes to the grave of a saint, the thicker becomes the swarm of the dead. … Above ground the thing was even worse—particularly in the great basilica [built in cemeteries]. … Every foot of ground before and behind the *confessio* and all around it was filled up with the dead. Sometimes whole layers of them extended over the entire length of the floor-space.[14]

It is no surprise, therefore, to discover that after Constantine's accession in 313, relic worship flourished most in regions where previously—during the first, second, and third centuries—Christians protected their dead from putrefaction.

Meanwhile, North African theologians formulated doctrines compatible with the traditional mortuary practices in their jurisdictions. The bishops focused chiefly on the correlation between celibacy and resurrection of the flesh. For example, Tertullian (160–220), bishop of Carthage and the first Church historian to write in Latin, argued that "just as it is in no other flesh but one's own that we commit adultery or strive for continence, so the exact same flesh is raised at resurrection."[15] Saint Paul believed that "to sleep with a prostitute involved nothing else than becoming one flesh with her, as surely as Adam became one flesh with Eve" (1 Corinthians, 6:16).[16] But Paul did not suggest, as did Tertullian, that sinful acts are literally implanted in the sinner's flesh, *both* in this life and in the next. Paul's admonition that the fornicator became "one flesh" with the prostitute had only a metaphorical and spiritual connotation.

Tertullian's belief that sin *was* defilement of the flesh had all the marks of the piety prevalent in many sectors of the Silk Road. As he put it, "all reality is corporeal. Even the soul is composed of very fine particles."[17] The Bishop saw sin and putrefaction as a negative correlate to the correspondence between celibacy and healing. These views reappear in the

Gospel of Thomas and the other Gnostic documents discovered at Nag Hammadi (a topic to be discussed periodically throughout this chapter). Additionally, a peculiarly North African—and also a Silk Road—preoccupation with exorcism merits attention. For example, Augustine, Bishop of Hippo, argued that infant baptism is an exorcism. The baptismal rite casts out the demons and "unclean spirits" which inhabit and pollute the semen emitted in sexual intercourse. Indeed, argued Augustine, life itself is a sexually transmitted and incurable disease. His belief that a primal sin is sexually transmitted from one generation to the next also gave doctrinal support to Tertullian's view that the sins of the flesh are raised in the resurrected flesh. In sum, "sexuality and the grave stood one at each end of the life of every human being. Like two iron clamps, they delineated inexorably mankind's loss of the primal harmony of body and soul."[18]

North African theologians thought redemption was a physical apotheosis, a restoration of the body to its original harmony with the soul. Resurrection returns the redeemed sinner to the paradisiacal state enjoyed by Adam and Eve prior to the couple's disobedience to God and expulsion from the Garden of Eden. Paul compared Adam—"the man of flesh" who brought sin and death into the world—to Christ, the second Adam and man of spirit, who brought life (1 Corinthians: 15: 21–22). This polarity may be interpreted literally or metaphorically. Augustine's literal interpretation, his belief in the continuity of fleshly defilement into the afterlife, was also reasserted on the ritual plane in North African, Egyptian, and other Near Eastern funerary practices meant to preserve the bodily purity of the deceased. The faithful reenacted with a fierce literalness—albeit within a Christian framework—a pre-Christian intimacy with the dead. Assimilating ritual purity with the sanctified relics of saints, people professed a fervent belief in the resurrection of the "exact same flesh" they had inhabited while alive. Relic cults, burials *ad sanctos,* and a wish to enter into a physical intimacy with Christ in the fourth and fifth centuries were rooted in a previous and peculiarly regional pre-Christian effort to preserve the identity of the deceased by means of a common meal. The following section goes back to Alexander and Euhemerus to explain how the rise of empires complicated Christian beliefs relating to identity in this life and in the next.

Concepts of the Soul and Problems of Identity, from Alexander to Origen

Euhemerus announced his doctrine—that gods were really heros and kings who had received divine honors—while he was minister to Cassander (311–298), the Macedonian king who succeeded Alexander. Euhemerus advanced this maxim to legitimize the centrality of kingship recently established by Alexander. As mentioned earlier, Alexander stands at the culmination of a thousand-year tradition of world conquerors who had equated the free mingling of peoples with the liberation of the dead from local netherworlds. Somewhat later, beginning in the second century BCE, the "soul" (psyche)—the bearer of personal identity and the source of emotion—also entered heaven. Ultimately, Hellenistic kings, now reputed to be "friends of the gods," were alleged to have acted as "saviors" and "benefactors" to their people. The movement to assimilate the honors offered to heroes and kings with homage paid to the gods led to the joining of worldly empires to celestial kingdoms peopled by newly heroicized dead.

In the Hellenistic period the honorific usage of "savior" and "benefactor"—terms traditionally ascribed to world conquerors from at least Cyrus to Alexander—led people to think that kings and emperors may guarantee that what is done on earth is also accomplished in heaven. Conversely, the subsuming of the heavens within the boundaries of a political empire radically changed the relations of gods to one another. By the time of Jesus and Augustus, the kings and emperors who distributed gifts and favors through descending hierarchies of subordinate officials and benefactors reappear in the reorganized structures of celestial governments. National deities were thought to hold different positions in numerous hierarchies of satraps, governors, and other sundry officials, all of them in the service of a supreme god who ruled the cosmos.[19] According to an earlier Hebrew version of this theme, in the Book of Jubilees (15:30b–32), written in the second century BCE, Yahweh

> chose Israel that they might be a people for himself. And he
> sanctified them and gathered them from all the sons of man

because [there are] many nations and many people, and they all belong to him, but over all of them he caused spirits to rule so that they might lead them astray from following him. But over Israel he did not cause any angel or spirit to rule because he alone is their ruler and he will protect them and he will seek for them at the hand of his angels and at the hands of his spirits and the hand of all of his authorities so that he might guard them and bless them and they might be his and he might be theirs henceforth.

The perceived simultaneity of deeds performed on earth with actions taken in heaven profoundly influenced the signification of names, and the relation of names to good and evil spirits. For example, in Mesopotamia, Palestine, and Egypt—where sin and sexuality were often identified with putrefaction—people associated a person's name with his or her body. Conversely, especially after Euhemerus, most Greeks believed that the soul was the bearer of identity and the seat of human emotion. In sum, ascription of personal identity to invisible beings—the soul or a spirit or a *daimon*—made it imperative to know the name of the spirit or demon one wished to invoke.

A Jewish philosopher, Philo of Alexandria (c. 20 BCE–c. 50 CE), thought that an incalculable number of invisible souls "fly and hover in the air." In the early third century (CE) the Greek Church Father, Origen of Alexandria—a famous Hellenistic center of Greek culture—wrote an essay on the subject of names, probably to refute Latin theologians who argued that names merely denote; they do not refer to essential traits of the owner.[20] In response to these assertions, Origen found it deplorable that

there are some who suppose that names are merely conventional and have no relation in nature to the things for which the names stand. And so they think there is no difference whether a person says "I worship the first god" or "Dios" or "Zeus" ... They must be told that the subject of names is something very deep and recondite and that if names were merely conventional, then the demons or any other invisible powers when summoned would not obey those who know their names and name the names that have been given. But as it is, certain sounds and syllables and expressions, aspirated or unaspirated and with a long or short vowel, when they are spoken aloud, by some unseen nature immediately bring us those who are summoned.[21]

This passage virtually paraphrases the Vedic practice of ritual speech to name the gods and give them existence.

Teaching in Alexandria, Origen shared the belief with Tertullian, Augustine, and other North African theologians that a primal sin is sexually transmitted from one generation to the next. They all equated sin with putrefaction. To my knowledge, however, only Origen, no one else, applied this teaching to show the purity of Jesus's tomb. "Just as his [Jesus's] birth was purer than all other births in that he was born not of sexual intercourse but of a virgin; so also his burial had the purity which was symbolically shown by the fact that his body was put away in a newly made tomb; this was not built of unhewn stones without any natural unity, but consisted of one rock all of one piece which was cut and hewn."[22]

Secondary Burial and Relic Cults Are Specific to Widely Separated Time Periods

The Synoptic Gospels were written long before people buried their dead near the tombs of the saints they worshipped. Matthew, Mark, and Luke describe Jesus as an exorcist. He cured disease and healed infirmities by casting out demons and "unclean spirits" from the bodies of people suffering from these afflictions. At the turn of the millennium many Palestinian Jews practiced secondary burial. After inhumation and a subsequent decomposition, the remaining bones were exhumed, placed in a small stone or clay box called an ossuary, and removed to a bone chamber. The biblical phrase, "to sleep with [or to be gathered to] one's ancestors" refers to secondary burial in a family tomb. Meanwhile, Jews in the Dispersion often sent the exhumed bones for reburial at Beth Shearim and other *public* cemeteries in Palestine.[23]

Subsequently, two centuries after the appearance of the Synoptic Gospels, burial practices conformed to an entirely different belief system. The exorcisms Jesus performed in Matthew, Mark, and Luke were now supplanted by miracles ascribed to the relics of saints; and burials *ad sanctos* supplanted the secondary interments that were common to a previous age. Moreover, demons were ubiquitous. Previously, according to the Synoptic Gospels, demons only inhabited the bodies of *living* people. Two centuries later, after the introduction of burials *ad sanctos,* putrefaction signified that demons had invaded human bodies after death. In sum, demons acquired timeless attributes when the doctrine of original sin and a belief assimilating sin with the putrefaction became widespread in the second century.

Return for a moment to the *Gospel of Thomas* and the 114 sayings allegedly recorded by the Apostle Judas Thomas (thought to be Jesus's twin brother and also Founder of the Church of the East). Written about the year 100, the document represents Syriac spirituality when Christians had only a small foothold in Syria. At that time, Edessa (modern Urfa) was both the spiritual capital of Syriac Christianity and a major mercantile center at the junction of a network of caravan routes to India. Located between the Euphrates and Tigris rivers in Northern Mesopotamia, Edessa stood at the convergence of two ancient routes—one from Armenia to Syria; the other from the Mediterranean to Iran, India, and China.

The Gospel of Thomas points to the differences that separated regions dominated by the figure of Jesus of Nazareth from other lands where people worshipped Jesus's twin brother, Thomas. The concept of martyrdom stood at the center of this dispute. Martyrs were Christians who died for their faith at the hands of Roman oppressors. And Jesus of Nazareth, not his twin brother, was the first Christian martyr. No Christians died for their faith in Northern Mesopotamia, nor did Christian martyrs appear in any other location east of the Euphrates until the year 300. The powers to heal and to exorcise demons ascribed to Jesus in the Synoptic Gospels were attributes ascribed at first to martyrs; during the second century these powers were transferred to the relics of countless saints who had died at the hands of the Romans in Africa, Palestine, Egypt, and in neighboring lands. In contrast, the *Gospel of Thomas* refers to no physical miracle, makes no mention of Jesus's crucifixion, and says nothing about his bodily resurrection. As Harold Bloom puts it, "unlike the canonical gospels, the gospel of Judas Thomas the Twin spares us the crucifixion, makes the resurrection unnecessary, and does not present us with a God named Jesus."[24]

The first stories associated with a relic cult in Syriac Christianity appear about the turn of the third century in a document entitled *The Acts of Thomas.* The text is a full-blown romance, describing Thomas's mission and martyrdom in India. The story ends with a report that Thomas's relics were translated from India to Edessa. In fact, a cult to Thomas's relics actually flourished at Edessa near the turn of the third century—about the time *The Acts of Thomas* was composed. Very different types of relic cults are at issue here. As mentioned earlier, explicitly Christian relic cults did not exist when the Synoptic Gospels were written, in the years between 70 and 90. At that time, Matthew, Mark, and Luke were perceived as Jewish documents; and specifically Christian martyrs were still unknown. Ignatius (c. 35–c. 107), Bishop of Antioch, and Polycarp (c. 69–c. 155), Bishop of Smyrna, may be associated with the earliest Christian relic cults. But cults to the relics of a Christian martyr are a second-century phenomenon.

The Acts of Thomas was composed in Nisibis, a trade route center about 130 miles east of Edessa. The document's origin in Nisibis explains why no miracle stories survive from the earlier relic cult in Edessa. In other words, people venerated Thomas's relics at Edessa *before* the apocryphal tales of his mission to India were written.[25] The belated connection made between Edessa and *The Acts of Thomas* not only moves the cult of Thomas's relics to an earlier date (about 180 or 190), but the transfer of the story—about Thomas's martyrdom in India—from Nisibis to Edessa also testifies to the missionary function of Thomas's relics. When seen from this perspective, the reputed translation of the Apostle's relics from India to Edessa in *The Acts of Thomas* suggests an early recognition of Edessa's spiritual supremacy. Even today Christians in South India not only claim an association with the Apostle Thomas, but they also continue to use Syriac as a liturgical language. Moreover, from the third century onward, "books and records treasured by Eastern and Western Christians recount" that, after reaching India, the Apostle St. Thomas had "gone on to China." In fact, the Syriac language inscribed on the "Stone of the Church of the East" in Chang-an (modern Xian) may date from the seventh century. The use of Syriac in the liturgy from Mesopotamia and Persia to India and China suggests that "the entire Church of the East used Syriac as its sacred language."[26]

No reference to martyrs or to martyrdom appears in the history of Syriac Christianity's expansion to India and China. In contrast, both the idea and the act of martyrdom are associated with Tatian, a student of Justin Martyr (c. 100–c.165). Justin and some of his disciples were denounced as Christians about the year 165. On refusing to sacrifice to the Emperor, they were scourged and beheaded. Shortly after Justin's martyrdom, Tatian wrote the *Diatessaron*—a history of the life of Christ compiled from the four canonical gospels *and also* from the *Gospel of Thomas*. Tatian's so-called harmony of the gospels remained "virtually the only version of the gospels in use among Syriac-speaking Christians for nearly 250 years."[27] The Church of Persia accepted the "gospel harmony"—which they called *Teachings of the Apostles*—"from about the end of the second century to the start of the sixth." And throughout this period the *Diatessaron* "became more popular [in Persia] than the [canonical] Gospels."[28]

The *Diatessaron* appeared only two generations after the *Acts of Thomas*. Although little is known about his career, Tatian's closeness to Justin Martyr, on the one hand, and the *Diatessaron*'s enormous popularity, on the other, established a close connection between Justin's martyrdom in Rome and Thomas's relics at Edessa. When Tatian returned to Northern Mesopotamia in 172 he reputedly founded the ascetic sect of Encratites. The Encratites were allegedly a Gnostic sect. Scholars cannot define a specifically "Christian Gnosticism" nor can they interpret the more general term, "Gnosticism." Everyone agrees that: (1) Gnosticism took many different forms; and (2) each form of Gnosticism is associated with the names of particular teachers such as Valentinus (second century); Basilides (who taught at Alexandria in the second quarter of the second century); or Marcion (died c. 160).

Moreover, scholars also agree that the *Gospel of Thomas* is of Gnostic provenance. Since Tatian included the *Gospel of Thomas* in the *Diatessaron,* the "Gospel Harmony" also falls into the Gnostic category. To my knowledge, scholars never refer to a Gnostic martyr. Yet, Tatian's close association with Justin Martyr and the importance of Jesus's twin brother, Thomas, in the *Diatessaron* make Justin—the first martyr associated with Syria—stand alongside Jesus as a victim of Roman persecution. Just as Thomas's relics at Edessa signified that Thomas stood toward India as his brother Jesus did toward Rome, so the *Diatessaron* stood toward the Church of the East in the same way the New Testament gospels stood toward the Church of Rome.

Buddhism, Gnosticism, and Manichaeism: Silk-Road Syncretisms

The term *docetism* refers to a belief in the early Church that the humanity and sufferings of the earthly Christ were merely apparent, not real. More specifically, docetic figures were fleshless beings perceived to have human form. The popularity of this teaching, which effectively denied Jesus's martyrdom, reached its zenith among Gnostics. Before pursuing this esoteric teaching any further, turn for a moment to Buddhism. A dictionary entry for *Nirmana-kaya*—the Buddha's emanation body—states that this concept may have originated in an early school of Buddhism, called the *Mahasamghika,* founded about 300 BCE. Like the later Mahayana school, this earlier group believed the Buddha "was essentially eternal and primordially enlightened in his cosmic or *dharma-kaya* aspect." But the Buddha also had the ability "to [become] manifest in various forms appropriate to different beings in *samsara*"[29]—the cycle of repeated birth and death that individuals undergo until they regain nirvana, the end of cyclic existence. The bodies of the Buddha are manifestly docetic, and they appear in both early and later Mahayana teachings.

Christian notions of docetism are not usually so specific, and they merit more attention. Consider the following definition taken from a glossary appended to a book about Gnosticism and Christianity:

> **Docetism.** From Greek "to seem," refers to the view that the Savior (Christ) only appeared in human form but was not a mortal human being. Docetic accounts of the crucifixion depict the Savior departing from the human body before it was hung on the cross.[30]

A longer entry in *The Encyclopedia of Religion* defines docetism as a denial of "the reality of Christ's physical incarnation." Although no evidence suggests the existence of a single sect of docetists, all authorities agree: (1) that docetic writings were numerous; and (2) the disputes and conflicting notions about docetism in the second century are too numerous to itemize. Yet, one fact seems indisputable: "images of Christ as a polymorphous divine being were common in the second century" *(Encyclopedia of Religion).*

Polymorphous images of divine beings—such as Bodhisattvas—are notoriously familiar figures in Buddhist writings. The parallel is certain. Bearing this analogue in mind, compare the Bodhisattva vow *(pranidhana)* with the Christian concept of redemption. According to the *Dictionary of Buddhism,* the Bodhisattva vow is:

> The aspiration or resolution undertaken by a Bodhisattva at the outset of his spiritual career. This resolution includes a vow to liberate all beings before he himself enters nirvana and leaves the world.

A.L. Basham cites the following passage from the Mahayana canon to show that the Bodhisattva's compassion and his willingness to endure suffering for the salvation of all living beings is sometimes expressed in almost explicitly Christian terms:

> I take upon myself ... the deeds of all beings, even those in the hells, in other worlds, in the realms of punishments.... I take their suffering upon me, ... I bear it, I do not draw back from it, I do not tremble at it, ... I have no fear of it, ... I do

not lose heart.... I must bear the burden of all beings, for I have vowed to save all things living, to bring them safe through the forest of birth, age, disease and rebirth. I think not of my own salvation, but strive to bestow on all beings the royalty of supreme wisdom. So I take upon myself all the sorrows of all beings. I resolve to bear every torment in every purgatory of the universe. For it is better that I alone suffer than the multitude of living beings. I give myself in *exchange*. I *redeem* the universe from the forest of purgatory, from the womb of *flesh,* from the realm of death. I *agree* to suffer as a **ransom** for the sake of all beings. Truly, I will not abandon them. For I have resolved to gain supreme wisdom for the sake of all that lives, to save the world [italics and bold type added].

At the end of this passage, Basham explains that "the idea of a Suffering Savior may have existed in the Middle East before Christianity, but ideas like this are not attested in Buddhism until after the beginning of the Christian era." Pointing out how closely the Suffering Bodhisattva resembles "the Christian conception of the God who gives his life as a ransom for the many," Basham goes on to say that "we cannot dismiss the possibility that the doctrine was borrowed by Buddhism from Christianity, which was vigorous in Persia from the 3rd century on."[31]

The reference to Persia points, once again, to the *Diatessaron,* known as *The Teachings of the Apostles* in Persia. We saw that from the end of the second century to the start of the sixth the *Diatessaron* was more popular among the Persians than the canonical Gospels. Scholars also find extensive parallels between the copy of the *Gospel of Thomas* found in the Nag Hammadi documents and a later devotional text in Manichaean literature. They think these analogues "may substantiate a connection between the *Gospel of Thomas* and a later gospel [written in the third century] in use among the Manichaeans."[32] Mani (c. 216–276) was born near Seleucia-Ctesiphon, the capital of the Persian Empire. Whatever version of the *Gospel of Thomas* the Manichaeans used, Tatian's inclusion of a *Gospel of Thomas* in the *Diatessaron* and Mani's Persian origins return us to the Silk Road and the Church of the East.

Several belief systems bore Mani's name in the third century. In the eastern sectors of the Silk Road, Manichaeism took the form of Buddhism or Taoism. In contrast, Mani's name appeared under Christian auspices on the western trade routes. To the east, in Central Asia and China, Mani's followers often saw him as Maitreya, the promised Buddha of the future. Others saw Mani as a Taoist deity. To the west, chiefly in North Africa and Rome, Manichaeans, who usually identified themselves as Christians, believed that Mani was the Holy Spirit. In Mani's lifetime polymorphous images of divine beings populated all sectors of the trade routes. An astonishing collection of parables, hymns, narratives, and prayers—published in a book entitled *Gnosis on the Silk Road*—illustrates Mani's merger of Gnostic Christianity with the radical religious dualism of Zoroaster. As this movement spread along the Silk Road from Turkey to Asia the cult acquired prominent features from Hinduism and Buddhism.[33]

In the western trade routes the concept of a "pleroma" was closely connected with the pervasive presence of fleshless beings perceived to have human form. The term first appears in the translations of the Septuagint, the most influential of the Greek versions of the Hebrew Bible. At that time (c. 132 BCE) "pleroma" signified fullness, totality, and perfection. The term acquired a theological content in the works of a famous scholar, Philo of Alexandria (c. 20 BCE–c. 50 CE). Philo's religious writings were numerous and also remarkably eclectic. Philo projected Stoic elements into the word "pleroma" in his development of an allegorical interpretation of Scripture. This usage was then taken up by both Christian and Gnostic schools. According to the Gnostics, *pleroma* "meant the entire divine, celestial dimension in its multiplicity and unity, which contains in itself the invisible, transcendent beings and their point of origin and goal of return as a place of rest in a state of salvation."[34] With a few minor modifications this sentence could also serve as a definition of redemption for the peripatetic holy men traveling on the trade routes extending from Persia and India into China.

Religious and Mercantile Exchange
from Mani to the Four Christian Gospels

Saint Augustine had been a Manichaean adept for ten years before he converted to Christianity. Afterwards, as bishop Hippo, Augustine discovered that "one of his deacons had even continued to attend Manichaean services as a 'Hearer'." Another young Manichaean decided to join Augustine's monastery after reading the *Diatessaron*.[35] Uneducated people were also attracted to Manichaeism. According to Peter Brown, the movement continued to attract many small men, largely respectable artisans and merchants, until outside forces led to the cessation of commerce. In fact, merchants "were the most effective missionaries of Manichaeism." But after the Mongols destroyed the "great commercial empires of the oases of the Gobi desert," Manichaeism "soon flickered out" in Central Asia. In the Roman Empire also, "the spread of Manichaeism may well have come to a halt with the cessation of commerce."[36]

Return for a moment to the legends of King Milinda (Menander), who ruled Bactrian Greece from 155 to 130 BCE. Menander's conversion to Buddhism, along with the fact that Plutarch recorded his legends in the late first century CE, may explain why Menander is the only Indo-Greek king to be celebrated in Indian literature. In his account of the disposition of Menander's remains, Plutarch claims that the cities of Bactria initially celebrated Menander's funeral according to Greek customs. But after these ceremonies, the cities allegedly "put forth rival claims [over possession of his relics] and only with difficulty came to terms, agreeing that they should divide the ashes equally and go away [with the reliquaries] and should erect monuments [statues] to him [Menander] in all their cities" (*Moralia* X, 821).

The alleged division of Menander's ashes among the cities reenacts, in the Bactrian trade centers, the legend of the division of the Buddha's bodily remains among rival Indian claimants who built stupas for his relics. Legend also recounts that King Ashoka controlled all 84,000 stupas of the Buddha. Since no images were venerated on the subcontinent during

Ashoka's reign (c. 268–c. 232 BCE), the so-called monuments or statues of Menander could not have been erected in India. However, image worship was a common practice in most Hellenistic cities. And Greek Buddhists erected an early statue of the Buddha, perhaps the first one, in the form of the God Apollo, at Gandhara in northwest India, about the time the earliest portions of the *Milindapanha* were composed. And this was also about the time Plutarch wrote about the distribution of Menander's cremated remains. This Indo-Greek confusion about how King Milinda was interred—stemming from very different notions about the protocol for royal funerary ceremonies—explains why, according to A.K. Narain, people on the subcontinent "traditionally associate Milinda with the origin of the Buddha image and [with] the construction of stupas."[37]

In Plutarch's world "good kings" reputed to have made great benefactions were honored for enjoying a friendship with the gods. The term "Friend" was also an official court title in Hellenistic kingdoms; and appointment to this office, often entitling the incumbent to large estates, placed the "Friend" among the King's closest advisors.[38] As mentioned earlier, Hellenistic monarchs who professed to stand toward their deities as did the officials who stood near their royal persons often inscribed the legend *Soter* (savior) on coins carrying portrait images of their persons. The historical Menander, having never set foot in Greece, had no image of a human face stamped on his coins, but the money did carry the inscription *Soter*.

Claims to "friendship" with the gods go back to Euhemerus of Messene (c. 345–c. 280 BCE), a Greek (Macedonian) collector of myths active in the decades immediately following the death of Alexander the Great (356–323 BCE). According to the doctrine that bears his name, *Euhemerism,* myths are really reports about early historical persons. For example, gods and heroes were at one time kings and heroes who acquired divine status. After death they became "friends of the gods" in recognition for their great benefactions to mankind. Indo-Greek kings hailed Alexander as an especially renowned Friend of the gods. And their Euhemerism is reflected in the titles on Ashoka's Rock edicts. These laws repeatedly refer to the King as "a friend of the gods." They also refer to Ashoka's gracious "mien"—a title that may have likened the beneficence shown by the royal visage to the power of the Buddha's smile. The kings portrayed on Hellenistic coins do not smile. For they represent the organized selfishness of nations. In contrast, the Buddha's smile communicates spiritual powers and a divinely inspired love.

Commerce and the Cross-Cultural Expansion of the Religious Imagination

Seventy-seven years ago a scholar showed that a tale of a lay disciple who walks on the water while on his way to visit the Buddha appears in a Christianized form in the first Gospel (Matthew 14: 22–31).[39] Buddhist and Christian elements often mixed easily among the more pious merchants who owned or who were entrusted with merchandise stored in the caravans traveling between India and Palestine. Religious beliefs communicated by people engaged in overland trade sometimes led ordinary people to draw unexpected religious implications from ordinary domestic transactions. For example, consider the apocryphal tale of a prostitute who by an "Act of Truth" made the Ganges flow backwards. Describing Ashoka's astonishment and outrage at this report, the author of this legend—recounted in the *Milindapanha*—has the Emperor ask the prostitute,

> "By what authority is it that you, insignificant as you are, have been able to make this mighty river flow backwards?" ... She replied: "It is by the power of Truth, great King." But the king said: "How can that power be in you—you, a woman of wicked and loose life devoid of virtue, under no restraint, sinful, who have overstepped all limits and are full of transgression, and live on the plunder of fools?"
>
> "It is true, O king, what you say. That is just the kind of creature I am. But even in such a one as I so great is the power of an Act of Truth that I could turn the whole world of gods and men upside down by it."

Then the king [asked]: "What is this Act of Truth?"

In a statement resembling a passage from a modern book on business ethics, the prostitute replied that she treats every customer equally—be he a noble or a brahman or a tradesman or a servant. Neither fawning to the first nor showing disdain toward the latter, "I do service to him who has bought me. This, your Majesty, is the basis of the Act of Truth by the force of which I turned the Ganges back" (IV, 1: 47–48).

Technically, a truth act, an ancient institution, is a speech-act "distinguishable from other closely related speech-acts in Vedic, such as oaths, vows, confessions, curses, blessings, charms, etc." In Vedic contexts, an act of truth is, above all, "an assertion of personal authority." In other words, an act of truth is performative in that its very utterance accomplishes the act which it designates—such as an exchange of wedding vows.[40] According to the *Milindapanha,* only a miracle so powerful as to make the Ganges flow backwards could justify the prostitute's performance of an act of truth in defiance of Emperor Ashoka, the first king to exercise sovereignty over almost all of India. The contrast between Vedic acts of truth and the prostitute's extraordinary transformation of this ritual act may be compared to the contrary significations between the face of a king imprinted on a coin and the Buddha's smile.

Final Reflections and Overview

The American poet Walt Whitman probably knew little or nothing about the Buddha. Yet two lines from his poem, *Song of Myself,* tell us a great deal about the meaning of the Buddha's smile:

> Whatever degrades another degrades me
> And whatever is done or said returns at last to me.[41]

The message conveyed by the Buddha's smile and the beauty and meaning found in literature are both notable for a temporal continuity. Timeless elements also apply to the Christian term *charism*—a word referring to a practice established by Saint Benedict (c. 480–c. 550) at the time he founded the Benedictine order.

Long after Benedict's demise, religious orders such as the Franciscans, Dominicans, Carmelites, Jesuits, etc., were organized according to principles prescribed by Saint Benedict. The members of every religious order are inspired and governed by the unique set of spiritual gifts transmitted by the Founder to his successors. For example, Saint Francis of (1181/2–1226) provided a sanctified code of conduct (also a formal canonical rule of life) which—believed to be inspired by the Holy Spirit—"was approved by the Church, and formally bestowed upon anyone who would consecrate themselves (by vows of poverty, chastity, and obedience) to follow the Franciscan way of life as a monk or a nun before a church authority." Thus entry into the Franciscan order gave monks and nuns "access to the Founder's spiritual gift. They would [both] receive and transmit Francis's charism: a special identification with the poor and [also] a joy in God's creation."[42]

A charism transmits a common state of mind and a defined way of life from one generation to the next. A shared or collective state of mind persisting over many generations points to a spiritual immanence comparable to the immanence believed to reside in Christ's living presence in the Eucharist. Just as the capacity for self-directed behavior defines an individual's personality, so a traditional practice having the power to organize the conduct of a religious community over an indefinite period of time confers a distinctive personality on a collectivity conceived to be immortal.

Moreover, in medieval rural communities parishes often functioned as lay counterparts to monastic and clerical charisms. For example, consider a village in southern France during the fifteenth century; where "the essential bond was locality: common labour, common worship; intermarriage formed its elements."[43] The religious unit, the parish, not only "doubled the community," but, as the village of Vignolles shows, the parish continued to function even after war had killed all but five villagers. The five survivors carried off to Bordeaux the silver cross "which belonged to their church in the time they lived there." After settling in different parishes in Bordeaux, the survivors assembled together, "and had a council and deliberation between themselves in 1417; and decided to give the cross to the *confrèrie* of Notre Dame in the parish of St.-Surin in Bordeaux on condition that

> the confrères should celebrate to solemn general anniversaries, with sung mass of requiem, each year in perpetuity for them and for the souls of those who had paid for the cross in the parish church of Vignolles. The village might have died; but the obligations of its community toward those who had provided for their cross continued to be observed some fifty miles away in Bordeaux.[44]

The cross functioned as a charism for the erstwhile community of Bordeaux. The five members seem to have been motivated by sentiments strangely similar to those voiced in the first stanza of a poem by Emily Dickinson:

> Because I could not stop for death—
> He kindly stopped for me—
> The Carriage held but just Ourselves—
> And Immortality.[45]

Endnotes

Notes to Introduction

1   Guy E. Swanson, *Religion and Regime: A Sociological Account of the Reformation* (Ann Arbor, MI: University of Michigan Press, 1967), pp. 1–13.

2   Christopher Tilley, *Metaphor and Material Culture* (Oxford, England: Blackwell, 1999), pp. 7–8.

3   Ed. Joseph P. McDermott (Cambridge, England: Cambridge University Press: 1999), p. 10.

4   I owe this information to my friend and colleague Whalen Lai.

5   Richard Huntington and Peter Metcalf, *Celebrations of Death: The Anthropology of Mortuary Ritual* (Cambridge, England: Cambridge University Press: 1979), p. 186.

6   *Lincoln at Gettysburg, The Words that Remade America* (New York: Simon and Schuster, 1992), p. 145.

7   *The Almanac of American History*, ed. Arthur M. Schlesinger, Jr. (New York: Perigee Books, 1983), p. 23.

8   Nicole Loraux, *The Invention of Athens. The Funeral Oration in the Classical City* (Cambridge, MA: Harvard University Press, 1986). See especially p. 20 and note 6.

9   *The Honey and The Hemlock. Democracy and Paranoia in Ancient Athens and Modern America* (Princeton, NJ: Princeton University Press, 1991), p. 17.

10   The adage appears at the top of the first page in Morris Berman, *The Twilight of American Culture* (New York: W.W. Norton, 2000).

11   Amitai Etzioni, in *Repentance, A Comparative Perspective,* eds. Amitai Etzioni and David Carney (Lanham, MD: Rowman & Littlefield, 1997), p. 5.

12   Francoise Meltzer, "Unconscious," *Critical Terms for Literary Studies*, eds. Franklin Lentricchia and Thomas McLaughlin, 2nd ed. (Chicago: University of Chicago Press, 1995), p. 147.

13   Although the Statue of Liberty and the image of Uncle Sam are both symbolic figures, only Uncle Sam shows distinctive personality traits. This characteristic defines an "organological analogy."

[14] *Thomas Jefferson, Author of America* (New York: Harper Collins, 2005), p. 3.

[15] Gordon S. Wood, *The American Revolution: A History* (New York: Modern Library, 2002), pp. 132–133).

[16] Philip Melling, *Fundamentalism in America: Millennialism, Identity, and Militant Religion* (Edinburgh University Press, 1999), p. 5. See also the report of the speech of Dr. Fred Bush, of the Fuller Theological Seminary, printed in the 2005 Annual Dinner Report of the Inter-Faith Peace Ministry of Orange County. I thank Deacon Rex Ehling, a long-time friend, for giving me a copy of this document.

[17] Michael Saso, "The Taoist body and cosmic prayer," in *Religion and the Body*, ed. Sarah Coakley (Cambridge, England: Cambridge University Press, 1997), p. 233.

[18] Steven Shankman, "These Three Come Forth Together, But Are Differently Named: Laozi, Zhuangzi, Plato," *Early China/Ancient Greece, Thinking through Comparisons*, eds. Steven Shankman and Stephen W. Durant (Albany, NY: State University of New York, 2002), p. 78.

[19] Donald R. Howard, *Writers and Pilgrims, Medieval Pilgrimage Narratives and Their Posterity* (Berkeley, CA: University of California Press, 1980).

[20] J. Thomas Rimer, *Pilgrimages, Aspects of Japanese Literature and Culture* (Honolulu: University of Hawaii, 1988).

[21] William R. LaFleur, *The Karma of Words. Buddhism and the Literary Arts in Medieval Japan* (Berkeley, CA: University of California Press, 1983), p. 4.

[22] Pei-Yi Wu, *The Confucian's Progress. Autobiographical Writings in Traditional China* (Princeton, NJ: Princeton University Press, 1990), p. 13.

[23] Richard Hooker, *Of the Laws of Ecclesiatical Polity*, Book I, chapter 10, section 10.9 (italics added). (Cambridge, MA, and London, England: The Belknap Press of Harvard University Press, 1977.)

NOTES TO CHAPTER I

Immanence and Language in the Formation of Individual and Collective Identity

[1] Guy E. Swanson, *Religion and Regime: A Sociological Account of the Reformation* (Ann Arbor: University of Michigan, 1967), p. 5.

[2] The passage is taken from Steven Shankman's chapter "Laozi, Zhuangzi, Plato," p. 16, in *Early China/Ancient Greece, Thinking through Comparisons*, eds. Steven Shankman and Stephen W. Durant (Albany, NY: State University of New York, 2002).

3 University of Chicago Press, 1987.

4 Ibid., pp. xii–xiii.

5 Ibid., p. xv.

6 Jeff Humphries, *Reading Emptiness: Buddhism and Literature* (Albany, NY: State University of New York, 1999), p. 6, italics added.

7 Ibid., p. 9.

8 Ibid., p. 7.

9 "The Chinese Attitude Toward the Past," *Papers on Far Eastern History,* vol. 39, March 1989, pp. 1–16.

10 Ibid., pp. 1–2.

11 Pei-Yi Wu, *The Confucian's Progress: Autobiographical Writings in Traditional China* (Princeton, NJ: Princeton University Press, 1990), p. 13.

12 Ibid.

13 James H. Foard, "Ippen and Pure Land Buddhist Wayfarers in Medieval Japan," in *The Pure Land Tradition: History and Development*, eds. James Foard, Michael Solomon, and Richard K. Payne (Berkeley, CA: Berkeley Buddhist Studies Series, 1996), pp. 357–389.

14 Karen Pechilis Prentiss, *The Embodiment of Bhakti* (Oxford University Press, 1999), p. 47.

15 Veena Das, *Structure and Cognition: Aspects of Hindu Caste and Ritual*, second ed. (Oxford and Delhi: Oxford University Press, 1992), p. 8.

16 Ibid., pp. 8–9.

17 Diana L. Eck, *A New Religious America: How a "Christian Country" Has Become the World's Most Religiously Diverse Nation* (San Francisco: Harper, 2001), p. 159.

18 Veena Das, *Structure and Cognition*, p. 8.

19 Jed Rubenfeld, *Freedom and Time: A Theory of Constitutional Self-Government* (New Haven, CT: Yale University Press, 2001), pp. 45–47.

20 Letter to Samuel Kercheval, 12 July 1816.

NOTES TO CHAPTER 2

Mormonism and Religious Diversity in the United States

1 "Preface on Names and Terms" in *The Book of J,* translated from the Hebrew by David Rosenberg. Interpreted by Harold Bloom (New York: Grove Widenfeld, 1990).

2 *The Encyclopedia of Religion*, ed. Mircea Eliade, (New York: Macmillan, 1987), entry: "Baptism."

3 University of Chicago, 1994, pp. 9 and 23–24.

4 Sabine MacCormack, "Loca Sancta: The Organization of Sacred Topography in Late Antiquity," in *The Blessings of Pilgrimage,* ed. Robert Ousterhout (Urbana and Chicago: University of Illinois Press, 1990), p. 17.

5 Douglas J. Davies, *An Introduction to Mormonism* (Cambridge, England: Cambridge University Press, 2003), p. 3.

6 Ibid., p. 251.

7 *The Cult of the Saints: Its Rise and Function in Latin Christianity* (Chicago: University of Chicago Press, 1981), p. 9.

8 *Western Society and the Church in the Middle Ages* (New York: Penguin Books, 1970), p. 30.

9 Douglas Davies, *An Introduction to Mormonism*, p. 4.

10 *The Anchor Bible Dictionary*, ed. in chief, David Noel Freedman (New York: Doubleday, 1992), entry: "Melchizedek."

11 Richard F. Burton, *The City of the Saints* (New York: Alfred A. Knopf, 1963), quoting Poet Laureate Robert Southey from March 1829 ("Sir Thomas More; or, Colloquies on the Progress and Prospects of Society," Vol. 1, Part 2, "The Reformation—Dissenters—Methodists").

12 Mitchell Merback, *The Thief, the Cross and the Wheel: Pain and the Spectacle of Punishment in Medieval and Renaissance Europe* (Chicago: University of Chicago Press, 1999), chapter 4.

13 This information is taken from an article in the *Los Angeles Times* by Rone Tempest, reprinted in the *San Francisco Chronicle*, Section: "California and the West" (Oct. 10, 2004).

14 Mitchell Merback, *The Thief, the Cross, and the Wheel*, p. 48.

15 *A New Religious America: How a "Christian Country" Has Become the World's Most Religiously Diverse Nation* (San Francisco: Harper, 2002).

16 Diana L. Eck, *A New Religious America*, p. 325.

17 James H. Foard, "Ippen and Pure Land Buddhist Wayfarers in Medieval Japan, in *The Pure Land Tradition: History and Development,* eds. James Foard, Michael Solomon, and Richard K. Payne (Berkeley, CA: Berkeley Buddhist Studies Series, 1996), p. 388.

18 George Lakoff, *Moral Politics: How Liberals and Conservatives Think,* 2nd ed. (Chicago: University of Chicago Press, 2002). See, above all, chapter 14, entitled "Two Models of Christianity."

[19] Ibid. See chapter 1, "Mind and Politics," especially the sections entitled "Common Sense and Uncommon Thoughts" and "Metaphorical Common Sense."

[20] *De l'Esprit*, 1758.

[21] See David S. Shields, *Civil Tongues and Polite Letters in British North America* (Chapel Hill, NC: University of North Carolina, 1997).

NOTES TO CHAPTER 3

Relics, Dreams, and Theater: Ancestor Cults and the Rise of World Religions

[1] Joseph R. Strayer, *On the Medieval Origins of the Modern State* (Princeton, NJ: Princeton University Press, 1970), p. 5.

[2] F.W. Mote, *Imperial China 900–1800* (Cambridge, MA: Harvard University Press, 1999), p. 9.

[3] Ibid., pp. 101–102.

[4] Ibid., p. 98.

[5] Robert Garland, *The Greek Way of Death* (Ithaca, NY: Cornell University Press, 1985), p. 75.

[6] H.W.F. Saggs, *The Might That Was ASSYRIA* (London: Sidgwick & Jackson, 1984), p. 114.

[7] Peter Brown, *The Cult of Saints* (Chicago: University of Chicago Press, 1981), cf. chapter 1, note 7, p. 88.

[8] *The Taoist Body* (Berkeley, CA: University of California Press, 1992), p. 166.

[9] Emily Ahern, *The Cult of the Dead in a Chinese Village* (Palo Alto, CA: Stanford University Press, 1973), pp. 161–174.

[10] Patricia Buckley Ebrey, "The Response of the Sung State to Popular Funeral Practices," in *Religion and Society in Tang and Sung China*, eds. Patricia B. Ebrey and Peter N. Gregory (Honolulu: University of Hawaii Press, 1993), pp. 209–240.

[11] I owe this information to conversations with Bruce Williams, a friend and colleague.

[12] Wu Hung, *The Wu Liang Shrine: The Ideology of Early Chinese Art* (Palo Alto, CA: Stanford University Press, 1989), p. 129.

[13] Mariko Namba Walter, "Buddhist Myth of Maudgalyayana (Mu-lien): Syncretism of South, Central and East Asian Beliefs in the Afterlife," in *Kalakalpa*, vol. 1, no. 1 (2003), pp. 79–103.

[14] Ellen Neskar, "Shrines to Local Former Worthies," in *Religions of China in Practice*, ed. Donald Lopez, Jr. (Princeton, NJ: Princeton University Press, 1996), p. 297.

15 *Imperial China 900 to 1800* (Cambridge, MA: Harvard University Press, 1999), p. 98.

16 Jean Dalby Clift and Wallace B. Clift, *The Archetype of Pilgrimage: Outer Action with Inner Meaning* (New York: Paulist Press, 1996), p. 33.

17 The citations are taken from a summary of Hertz's work in *The Dictionary of Anthropology*, ed. Thomas Barfield (Oxford, England: Blackwell, 1997), p. 109, column 2.

18 Jonathan Z. Smith, *Map is not Territory* (Leiden: Brill, 1978), p. 114, note 22.

19 Peter Brown, *The Cult of Saints*, p. 4. Cf. also p. 12, note 7.

20 Ibid., p. 12.

21 Ibid., p. 7.

22 Ibid., p. 90.

23 Charles Elliott, *Memory and Salvation* (London: Darnton, Longman, and Todd, 1995), p. 9.

24 Vol. 3, 1990, p. 521.

25 Princeton, NJ: Princeton University Press, 1989.

26 Ibid., pp. 7–8.

27 Ibid., p. 190.

28 Alan H. Somerstein, *Aeschylean Tragedy* (Bari, Italy: Levante Editions, 1996), p. 19.

29 Diane Ackerman, *An Alchemy of Mind* (New York: Scribner, 2004), p. 215.

30 Wendy Doniger O'Flaherty, *Dreams, Illusions, and Other Realities* (Chicago: University of Chicago Press, 1984), p. 260.

31 Ibid., p. 267.

32 John Brennan, "Dreams, Divination, and Statecraft: The Politics of Dreams in Early Chinese History and Literature," in *The Dream and the Text: Essays on Literature and Language,* ed. Carol Schreiber Rupprecht (Albany, NY: SUNY Press, 1993), pp. 73–102.

33 Berthold Laufer, "Inspirational Dreams in East Asia," in *Journal of American Folk-Lore*, vol. 44, April-June, 1931, no. 172, p. 210.

34 I owe this information to my friend and colleague Whalen Lai.

35 Ibid., pp. 210–211.

36 Entry, "Incubation."

37 Wendy Doniger O'Flaherty, *Dreams, Illusions and Other Realities,* p. 280.

NOTES TO CHAPTER 4

Germany: A History of Religious and Cultural Incoherence

1 By Eric A. Blackall, 2nd ed. (Ithaca, NY: Cornell University Press, 1978).

2 Norbert Elias, *The History of Manners* (New York: Pantheon Books, 1978), pp. 13–14.

3 *The Cambridge Dictionary of Philosophy*, ed. Robert Audi (Cambridge, England: Cambridge University Press, 1995), p. 243, col. 1.

4 London: Hutchingon's University Library, 1947.

5 For the comedy of errors behind this essay see H.J. Paton, "An Alleged Right to Lie from Benevolent Motives: A Problem in Kantian Ethics," in *Kant-Studien* vol. 45 (1953–54), pp. 190–203.

6 Gordon S. Wood, *The American Revolution: A History* (New York: Modern Library, 2002), p. 55.

7 *The Complete Works of St. Thomas More*, vol. 4 (New Haven, CT: Yale University Press, 1963), pp. 223–225.

8 Michel Despland, *La religion en occident: Evolution des idées et du vécu* (Montreal: Fides, 1979), p. 295.

9 *The Encyclopedia of Religion*, ed. Mircea Eliade (New York: Macmillan, 1987), entry: "Holy, Idea of the."

10 Ibid., p. 436.

11 Diarmaid MacCulloch, *The Reformation* (New York: Viking, 2003), p. 124.

12 Ibid., pp. 124–125.

13 Ibid., p. 126.

14 Ibid., pp. 122–127.

15 George G. Iggers, *The German Conception of History: The National Tradition of Historical Thought from Herder to the Present* (Middletown, CT: Wesleyan University Press, 1968), p. 20.

16 *Complete Works of Oscar Wilde*, ed. J.B. Foreman (London and Glasgow: Collins, 1967), p. 1,071.

17 The passage is from "Vorlesung gehalten am *Dies Akademicus von Werner Richter: Deutsche und Angelsächsische Universitätsideale," Bonner akademische Reden,"* vol. 8 (Bonn, 1953).

18 Palo Alto, CA: Stanford University Press, 1988.

19 Philip M. Soergel, *Wondrous In His Saints: Counter-Reformation Propaganda in Bavaria* (Berkeley, CA: University of California Press, 1993).

[20] William E. Monter, *Witchcraft in France and Switzerland: The Borderlands During the Reformation* (Ithaca, NY: Cornell University Press, 1969), pp. 190–191.

[21] New York: Henry Holt, 1999.

[22] "Popular Religion and Holy Shrines," in *Religion and the People*, ed. James Obelkevitch (Chapel Hill, NC: University of North Carolina Press, 1979), pp. 20–86. *Religious Practices and Collective Perceptions: Hidden Homologies in the Renaissance and Reformation,* the entire volume of *Historical Reflexions/ Reflexions Historique*, vol. 7 (1980). "German Holiness and Western Sanctity in Medieval and Modern History" in *Culture, Society, and Religion in Early Modern Europe. Essays by the Students and Colleagues of William J. Bouwsma,* ed. Ellery Schalk, *Historical Reflections/Reflexions Historique,* Spring 1988, vol. 14, no. 1.

[23] Pierre Delooze, *Sociology et canonizations* (La Haye, 1969), p. 201, note 1, reports that in the twelfth century a cardinal explained to abbé Gerard, who wanted to have the archbishop of Cologne canonized, that German territories only produced warriors; only a miracle could create a saint in these regions.

[24] Steven Ozment, *A Mighty Fortress: A New History of the German People* (San Francisco: Harper Collins, 2004), p. 40.

[25] *The Portable Medieval Reader*, ed. James B. Ross and Mary M. McLaughlin (New York: The Viking Press, 1963), pp. 420–421.

[26] See the section on Pomerania in the articles collected in: *Heidenmissionen und Kreuzzugsgedanken in der deutschen Ostpolitik des Mittelalters,* ed. Helmut Beumann (Darmstadt, 1973).

[27] Helmuth Heyden, *Kirchengeschichte Pommerns,* vol. I (Köln-Braunfels: R. Mueller, 1957), p. 146.

[28] *Western Society and the Church in the Middle Ages* (New York: Penguin Books, 1970), p. 253.

[29] L. Rothkrug, *Religious Practices and Collective Perceptions: Hidden Homologies in the Renaissance and Reformation,* the entire volume of *Historical Reflections/ Reflexions Historique,* vol. 7, 1980, p. 262.

[30] Caroline W. Bynum, *The Medieval History Journal,* vol. 7, no. 2 (2004), pp. 227–241.

[31] *Art and Architecture of Late Medieval Pilgrimage in Northern Europe and the British Isles,* eds. Sarah Blick and Rita Tekippe (Leiden and Boston: Brill, 2005), see pp. 590, 593, 595, note 24, and p. 633.

[32] Geoffrey Barraclough, *The Origins of Modern Germany* (New York: B. Blackwell, 1966), pp. 136ff.

[33] Herbert Moller, "The Social Causation of the Courtly Love Process," *Comparative Studies in Society and History,* vol. I (January 1959), p. 148. John B. Fried, "The Origins of the European Nobility: The Problem of the Ministerials," *Viator,* vol. 7 (1976), pp. 211–241 review the literature on ministerials.

[34] Georges Duby, "Dans la France du Nord-Ouest. Au XIIe siècle: les 'jeunes' dans la societé aristocratique," *Annales, Economies-Societés-Civilisations,* vol. 19 (1964), p. 840.

[35] Herbert Moller, "The Social Causation of the Courtly Love Process," pp. 148–149.

[36] Sidney Painter, *French Chivalry: Chivalric Ideas and Practices in Medieval France* (Ithaca, NY: Cornell, 1940), p. 87.

[37] On this subject see, John B. Fried, "The Origins of the European Nobility: The Problem of the Ministerials."

[38] Georg von Schierghofer, "Umrittsbrauch and Rossegen. Ein Beitrag zur vergleichenden Volkskunde unter Berücksichtigung Altbayerns," *Bayrische Hefte für Volkskunde,* vols. 1–4 (Munich, 1921). Rudolf Hindringer, *Weihross und Rossweihe. Eine Religionsgeschichtliche-volkskundliche Darstellung der Umritte, Pferdesegnungen und Leonhardifahrten im Germanishen Kulturkreis* (Munich: Lentner, 1932), p. 113.

[39] I.R. Schmidt, "Königsumritt und Huldigung in ottonischer-sälischer Zeit," *Vorträge und Forschungen,* vol. 6 (1961), pp. 114ff., 177ff.

[40] Wolfgang Bruckner, "Zur Phänomenologie und Nomenklatur des Wallfahrtswesens und seiner Erforschung, "*Volkskultur und Geschichte, Festgabe für Joseph Dunninger* (Berlin, 1970), p. 412, note 97.

[41] Bruno Neundorfer, "Zur Entstehung von Wallfahrten und Wallfahrtspatrozinen im mittelalterlichen Bistum Bamberg," *Bericht des historischen Kreises für die Pflege des ehemaligen Furbistums Bamberg,* vol. 99, p. 110. Also by the same author, "Wallfahrten zur hl. Katarina im Bistum Bamberg," ibid., vol. 102 (1966), p. 233.

[42] Christian Schreiber, ed. *Wallfahrten durchs deutsche Land. Eine Pilgerfahrt zu Deutschlands heiligen Stätten* (Berlin: Lentner, 1928), p. 257.

[43] Ernst Burgstaller and Adolf Helbok, eds., *Österreichischer Volkskundeatlas* (Linz: a.d. Donau, 1959), Map *Umritte,* drawn by Helmut Fielhauer.

[44] Schreiber, *Wallfahrten durchs deutsche Land,* p. 294.

[45] Rudolf Kriss, *Die Wallfahrtsorte Europas* (Munich: Lentner, 1950), pp. 55–56.

[46] On this subject see, above all, Siegfried Hoyer, "Die Armlederbewegungen in Bauernaufstand 1336–1339," *Zeitschrift für Geschichtswissenschaft* (1965), pp. 74–89.

⁴⁷ Wilhelm Volkert, "Die Juden in der Oberpfalze im 14. Jahrhundert," *Zeitschrift für bayerische Landesgeschichte*, vol. 30 (1967), pp. 161–200.

⁴⁸ Mitchell B. Merback, *The Thief, The Cross and the Wheel: Pain and the Spectacle of Punishment in Medieval and Renaissance Europe* (Chicago: University of Chicago Press, 1999), pp. 190–191.

⁴⁹ Eds. Sarah Blick and Rita Tekippe (Leiden and Boston: Brill, 2005).

⁵⁰ Chapter 23, pp. 587–646, and appended images.

⁵¹ Ibid., p. 587.

⁵² Ibid., p. 589.

⁵³ For an exhaustive study of this topic, see Kathy Stuart, *Defiled Trades and Social Outcasts: Honor and Ritual Pollution in Early Modern Germany* (Cambridge, England: Cambridge University Press, 2000).

⁵⁴ H.C. Erik Midelfort, "Heartland of the Witchcraze," *History Today*, vol. 31 (1981), p. 28.

⁵⁵ Kilian McDonnell, *John Calvin: The Church and the Eucharist* (Princeton, NJ: Princeton University Press, 1967), p. 190.

⁵⁶ *The Encyclopedia of Religion*, entry: "Holy, Idea of the."

⁵⁷ Gordon S. Wood, *The American Revolution*, p. 132.

⁵⁸ Philip Melling, *Fundamentalism in America*, p. 5.

⁵⁹ Ibid., p. 18.

⁶⁰ *The Encyclopedia of Religion*, ed. Mircea Eliade, vol. 3, pp. 32–33, entry: "John Calvin."

⁶¹ *Mary's Mother, Saint Anne in Late Medieval Europe* (Philadelphia: Pennsylvania State University Press, 2004), p. 1.

⁶² Ibid., pp. 17–18.

⁶³ Ibid., p. 20.

⁶⁴ Ibid., p. 49.

⁶⁵ William J. Bouwsma, *John Calvin: A Sixteenth-Century Portrait* (Oxford, England: Cambridge University Press, 1988), p. 167.

NOTES TO CHAPTER 5

World Religions, Commerce, and Religious Itinerants in the Age of Empires

¹ The historical Buddha died in either 486 BCE or 386 BCE.

² See the commentary to this passage in *The Search for the Authentic Words of Jesus: The Five Gospels*, eds. Robert W. Funk, Roy W. Hoover, and The Jesus Seminar (New York: Macmillan, 1993), pp. 234–235.

3 *Gnosis on the Silk Road: Gnostic Texts from Central Asia*, ed. Hans-Joachim Klimkeit (San Francisco: Harper, 1993).

4 *The Gospel of Thomas: Hidden Sayings of Jesus*, ed. Marvin Meyer, with an interpretation by Harold Bloom (San Francisco: Harper, 1992), saying 42 and note on p. 87.

5 Ibid., editor's note, p. 104.

6 John Renard, *Seven Doors to Islam: Spirituality and the Religious Life* (Berkeley, CA: University of California Press, 1996), p. 1.

7 *The Cult of Saints: Its Rise and Function in Latin Antiquity* (Chicago: University of Chicago Press, 1981), p. 10.

8 Ibid., pp. 90–91.

9 Editor's note to saying 16 explains that the term "alone" or *monachos,* which appears in sayings 16, 49, and 75, "may indicate one who is unique, solitary, or lonely, one who is unmarried or (later in a technical sense) a monk."

10 This section is adapted from my foreword to *Holy People of the World: A Cross-Cultural Encyclopedia,* ed. Phyllis Jestice (Santa Barbara, CA: ABC CLIO, 2004).

11 Pankaj Mishra, *An End to Suffering: The Buddha In the World* (New York: Farrar, Straus and Giroux, 2004), p. 45.

12 *The Oxford Companion to the Bible*, eds. Bruce M. Metzger and Michael D. Coogan (Cambridge, England: Oxford University Press, 1993), entry: "Ezekiel's Temple," p. 733, col. 1.

13 Peter Brown, *The Cult of the Saints*, p. 88.

14 I owe much of this information to my friend and colleague Phyllis Jestice.

15 Euripides, *Hippolytus*, 1437–1438.

16 "What is not in dispute is that the belief in the underworld did not go unchallenged in the Classical period and that a new idea grew up, probably in the first half of the fifth century, of the *psychai* of the dead being transported up to heaven." Robert Garland, *The Greek Way of Death* (Ithaca, NY: Cornell University Press, 1985), p. 75.

17 Cited by Walter Burkert, "The Meaning and Function of the Temple in Classical Greece," in *Temple and Society*, ed. Michael V. Fox (Winoa Lake, IN: Eisenbrauns, 1988), p. 39.

18 "Homeric dreamers spoke of *seeing* a dream, not of having one as modern dreamers do. The word that is usually used in Homeric texts to denote a dream is *oneiros,* which designates a dream-*figure* (not the more generalized dream-*experience*." Patricia Cox Miller, *Dreams in Late Antiquity: Studies in the Imagination of a Culture* (Princeton, NJ: Princeton University Press, 1994), p. 17.

[19] Ibid., pp. 17, 19.

[20] On this matter see two sections in Chapter Two: "Avoidance of Corpse Defilement: Double Burial and the Rise of World Religions" and "Dreams and Dream Figures in Cross-Cultural Perspective."

[21] So-called double graves are (1) extremely common; (2) they have been widespread for a long time; (3) today some "double graves" concern the interment of a corpse; (3) others involve a division of cremated ashes; (4) the dual burial of a corpse takes place over a 3- to 5-year period, in which the so-called second grave, a cenotaph, is built in a graveyard run by local Buddhist monks. The corpse remaining at all times in the original grave is located in a public cemetery; (5) Double burial of cremated ashes involves the division of ashes at two grave sites, one near home and the other at a national site, either near the tomb of a founder or close to a pilgrimage site on a sacred mountain.

[22] Steven Collins, *Nirvana and Other Buddhist Felicities: Utopias of the Pali imaginaire* (Cambridge, England: Cambridge University Press, 1998), p. 28.

[23] The other three were Isthmia, Olympia, and Nemea.

[24] Irad Malkin, *Religion and Colonization in Ancient Greece (Studies in Greek and Roman Religion 3)* (Leiden, England: Brill, 1987), p. 3.

[25] Ibid., pp. 129, 134.

[26] *The Oxford Companion to Classical Civilization,* eds. Simon Hornblower and Anthony Spawforth (Cambridge, England: Oxford University Press, 1998), p. 181.

[27] Jürgen Habermas, *The Structural Transformation of the Public Sphere: An Inquiry into a Category of Bourgeois Society* (Cambridge, MA: MIT Press, 1991), pp. 3–4.

[28] Walter Burkert, *Greek Religion* (Cambridge, MA: Harvard University Press, 1985), pp. 203–205.

[29] Arthur Darby Nock, "Soter and Evergetes," in *Essays on Religion and the Ancient World* (Cambridge, MA: Harvard University Press, 1984), vol. 2, pp. 720–735, citations taken from pp. 720, 721–722, 725–726.

[30] *Greek Religion*, pp. 298, 211.

NOTES TO CHAPTER 6

Silk-Road Pieties and the Rise of World Religions

[1] *From the Maccabees to the Mishnah* (Philadelphia: Westminster Press, 1987), p. 29.

[2] Except for female members of the royal family, no women were deported.

3 Donald Harmon Akenson, *Surpassing Wonder: The Invention of the Bible and the Talmud* (Chicago: University of Chicago Press, 1998), p. 71.

4 Louis H. Feldman, *Jew and Gentile in the Ancient World: Attitudes and Interactions from Alexander to Justinian* (Princeton, NJ: Princeton University Press, 1993), pp. 328–331.

5 Anthony J. Saldarini, *Matthew's Christian-Jewish Community* (Chicago: University of Chicago Press, 1994), p. 15.

6 Louis H. Feldman, *Jew and Gentile*, p. 29.

7 Harper San Francisco, 2004.

8 Ibid., p. 25.

9 Ibid., p. 36.

10 Ibid., p. 39. The rest of the chapter, pp. 39–68, is devoted to developing these themes at length.

11 *The Anchor Bible Dictionary*, entry: "Palmyra."

12 Paula Fredriksen, "Apocalypse and Redemption in Early Christianity from John of Patmos to Augustine of Hippo," *Vigilae Christianae*, vol. 45 (1991), p. 155.

13 Robert C. Gregg and Denis E. Groh, *Early Arianism: A View of Salvation* (Philadelphia: Fortress Press, 1981), p. 178.

14 F. Van der Meer, *Augustine The Bishop. The Life and Work of a Father of the Church* (London: Sheed and Ward, 1961), pp. 492–493.

15 *On Resurrection of the Flesh*, LIV; LIX.

16 Cited by Peter Brown, *The Body and Society: Men, Women, and Sexual Renunciation in Early Christianity* (New York: Columbia University Press, 1988), p. 51.

17 *On Resurrection of the Flesh*, p. 35.

18 Peter Brown, *The Body and Society*, p. 416.

19 In the introduction to his edition of *Origin Contra Celsum* (Cambridge, England: Cambridge University Press, 1953), Henry Chadwick explains that "even by the time of Philo [a contemporary of Jesus] … it was common enough to justify polytheistic practice by pleading that the local deities are as it were God's provincial administrators and governors. In the second century A.D. the notion is widespread. [From] the orations of Aelius Aristides, we learn that Zeus appoints administrators for the various regions of the world, like governors and satraps" (p. xix).

[20] Testimony from Pliny the elder (24–79 CE) suggests that in Rome only the uneducated believed in the efficacy of invoking names in ritual incantations: "Have words or formulated incantations any effect? ... As individuals ... all our wisest men reject belief in them, although as a body the public at all times believes in them unconsciously" (*Natural History,* XVIII, ii, 9, iii).

[21] *An Exhortation to Martyrdom,* XLIV.

[22] *Origen Contra Celsum,* article 69, p. 119.

[23] *The Oxford Companion to the Bible,* entry: "Burial Customs."

[24] "A Reading," *The Gospel of Thomas,* ed. Marvin Meyer (San Francisco: Harper, 1992), p. 111.

[25] George L. Huxley, "Geography in the *Acts of Thomas,*" in *Greek, Roman, and Byzantine Studies,* vol. 24, no. 1, pp. 71–80.

[26] Martin Palmer, *The Jesus Sutras: Rediscovering the Lost Scrolls of Taoist Christianity* (New York: Ballantine Publishing Group, 2001), p. 44.

[27] Ian Gillman and Hans-Joachim Klimkeit, *Christians in Asia Before 1500* (Ann Arbor: University of Michigan, 1999), p. 42.

[28] Martin Palmer, *The Jesus Sutras,* p. 103.

[29] Damien Keown, *Dictionary of Buddhism* (Cambridge, England: Oxford University Press, 2003), p. 194.

[30] Karen L. King, *What is Gnosticism?* (Cambridge, MA: Harvard University Press, 2003), p. 208.

[31] A. L. Basham, *The Wonder That Was India: A Survey of the Culture of the Indian Sub-Continent Before the Coming of the Muslims* (New York: Grove Press, 1954), pp. 275–276.

[32] *The Gospel of Thomas,* ed. Marvin Meyer, "Introduction," p. 6.

[33] *Gnosis on the Silk Road: Gnostic Texts from Central Asia,* translated and presented by Hans-Joachim Klimkeit (San Francisco: Harper, 1993).

[34] *Encyclopedia of the Early Church* (New York: Oxford University Press, 1992), entry: "Pleroma."

[35] Peter Brown, *Augustine of Hippo: A Biography* (Berkeley, CA: University of California Press, 1969), p. 55.

[36] Ibid.

[37] *The Oxford Classical Dictionary,* s.v. Menander.

[38] For the Ptolemies see L. Koenen, "The Ptolemaic King as a Religious Figure," *Images and Ideologies: Self Definition in the Hellenist Worlds,* eds. Anthony W. Bulloch et al. (Berkeley, CA: University of California Press, 1993), p. 30. For

the Seleucids, see *From Samarkand to Sardis: A New Approach to the Seleucid Empire*, eds. Susan Sherwin-White and Amelie Kuhrt (Berkeley, CA: University of California Press, 1993), pp. 132–133.

[39] William Norman Brown, *The Indian and Christian Miracles of Walking on the Water* (Chicago: Open Court, 1928), pp. 27ff., 47, 53, 61, 69, 71.

[40] George Thompson, "On Truth Acts in Vedic," *Indo-Iranian Journal 41*, 1998, pp. 125–126.

[41] The *Song of Myself* was always the centerpiece of the collection of poems *Leaves of Grass*, published in 1855 and repeatedly revised and expanded in eight editions. But the title poem, *Song of Myself*, dates from the 1888 edition.

[42] I owe this information to a colleague, Anthony Bellotti.

[43] P.S. Lewis, *Later Medieval France: The Polity* (New York: Saint Martins Press, 1968), p. 276.

[44] Loc. cit.

[45] "Because I Could Not Stop for Death." Emily Dickinson lived from 1830 to 1886.

Index

DATE DUE

GAYLORD No. 2333   PRINTED IN U.S.A.

Library Services